of prayer with

EUSEBE-HENRI MENARD

15 days
of prayer series

On a journey, it's good to have a guide. Even great saints took spiritual directors or confessors with them on their itineraries toward sanctity. Now you can be guided by the most influential spiritual figures of all time. The 15 Days of Prayer series introduces their deepest and most personal thoughts.

This popular series is perfect if you are looking for a gift, or if you want to be introduced to a particular guide and his or her spirituality. Each volume contains:

- ∽ A brief biography of the saint or spiritual leader
- ∽ A guide to creating a format for prayer or retreat
- ∽ Fifteen meditation sessions with focus points and reflection guides

15 days
of prayer with

EUSEBE-HENRI MENARD

Christian Rodembourg

TRANSLATED BY

FATHER ROBERT MORFESI, M.S.A.
SISTER MARY RYAN, F.D.L.P.

NEW CITY PRESS
Hyde Park, NY

Published in the United States by New City Press
202 Comforter Blvd., Hyde Park, NY 12538
www.newcitypress.com
©2011 New City Press (English translation)

This book is a translation of *Prier 15 Jours Avec Eusebe-Henri Menard*,
published by Nouvelle Cité, 2010, Montrouge, France

Imprimatur: Very Reverend Isaac C. Martinez Chuquizana, M.S.A.
General Animator of the Missionaries of the Holy Apostles,
General House, Montreal, June 25, 2009

Cover Photo: Archives of the General House
Cover design by Durva Correia

ISBN 978-1-56548-403-0

Printed in the United States of America

"He went up the mountain
and summoned those whom he wanted
and they came to him.
He appointed twelve
that they might be with him
and he might send them forth to preach ..."

(Mark 3:13–19)

To Simonne ALBERT and
André RODEMBOURG,
My parents.

To my confreres, Isaac, Jean-Paul, Roma
and to the friends who
encouraged me and advised me
while writing this book, thank you.

To Father Yves Begin, M.S.A. through whom
I came to know the Missionaries
of the Holy Apostles, thank you.

United in the Lord Jesus (CN §8).

C.R.

Contents

Who Is Father Eusebe-Henri Menard?

E usebe-Henri Menard, baptized Joseph-Henri-Pierre,[1] was born on January 6, 1916 in East Broughton (QC) to a family of eleven children, nine boys and two girls.[2] His parents, Charles Menard and Marie-Anna Labbe of humble origins, rooted in a profound faith in Divine Providence nurtured his dream to follow a religious and priestly vocation. In 1936, following his high school, he enrolled in theology at the Seminary of Foreign Missions (QC). On September 17, 1937, he joined the Franciscans of Lennoxville (QC) at the monastery of the Assumption. On September 18, 1941, he pronounced his solemn vows at the monastery of the Resurrection in Montreal. On September 28th that same year, he was ordained to the priesthood by Bishop Omer Plante.

---

1. In this text, *Père Eusèbe-Henri Ménard* will be called "Father Menard" and *Missionnaires des Saints Apôtres* will be referred to as "M.S.A." All the references are from the French edition, except the Spiritual Testament.
2. Paul Longpré, Eusèbe-Henri Ménard, un vrai fils de François (a true son of Francis), Fides, Montreal, 2000, p. 106.

Birth of a Founder

He shared his faith warmly and whole-heartedly. In 1943, because of his eloquent manner of transmitting the Word of God and his stunning ability to bring the Gospel to life, Father Menard was appointed preacher of retreats for the laity, priests and religious at Maison du Christ-Roi (House of Christ the King), near Montreal.

From 1943 to 1946, as he met businessmen, he discovered their great thirst to be apostles, that is, committed laymen in the Church. Repeatedly, he stressed that all baptized persons are called to holiness and that each person has his place in the Church. He also met young adults who declared their hope to become priests. Most of the time, because of their age and life journey till then, the doors to the seminary remained closed to them. In the 1940's, to become a priest, it was customary to sign up for Classical Studies beginning at age fourteen, and moving through the Minor to the Major seminary. At that time, there really wasn't room for another road to the priesthood.

Father Menard was acutely aware that these young adults were being blocked in their hope to become priests. He felt an intense calling to pray for these vocations, and decided to receive these young people and accompany them in both their human and spiritual growth. Providentially in 1946, the Work of the Holy Apostles was born with the founding of "École apostolique Saint-Pascal-Baylon" (Montreal). Its mission was to form priests and Christian laymen for the Church. Canonically, on March 25, 1956 this first foundation (S.SS.A.) became known as a Pious Union. In 1945, during a retreat, Father Menard met Mr. Hector Durand (1892–1972), a businessman from Montreal. Moved by the parable of the rich man and Lazarus (Lk 16:19–31), Mr. Durand along with his wife Claire Farrell gave a lot of time, talents and a large part of his fortune to the development of the Work of the Holy Apostles. A man of faith, charity and hope, a plain, honest man, and not always understood. He was a Spirit-filled man and a dedicated worker and Father Menard considered him the co-founder of the Work (CN #210). In the footsteps of Hector Durand, many lay people collaborated in the development of the apostolates of the Society. Long before Vatican II, Father Menard handed over the management of the assets and administrative responsibility of the apostolates of the Society to "Corporations and Foundations."

Multiplication of the Foundations

In 1950, Father Menard founded, with Sister Marie Toupin (1903–1972), the Society of the Sisters of the Holy Apostles of Canada. From 1952 to 1961, many apostolates, houses and seminaries were built or acquired: the Seminary of the Holy Apostles of Côte Sainte-Catherine (1952), Saint-Paul's Retreat House (1953), Holy Apostles Seminary in Cromwell, Conn. (1957), Saint-Jean-Vianney College (Montreal 1959). In 1960, a Canadian confrere initiated an apostolic work in the Amazon region of Peru. In 1961, Father Menard received the Marian Centre Marie-Reine-des-Coeurs in Chertsey. In 1962, he opened a scholastic college in Washington, D.C.

A Major Trial

The multiplication of these foundations became a great concern for the Church to the point that Cardinal Paul-Émile Léger, Archbishop of Montreal, made known his serious reservations. Cardinal Leger feared the human and financial repercussions that could surge up in the management of all these apostolates. Father Menard's youth and enthusiasm, in spite of his charism, do not make the events easier to live. In the heat of the ensuing dialogue, Father Menard was challenged by serious misunderstandings. In 1962, Father Menard was obliged to leave Montreal. This emotional departure, shortly before the beginning of Vatican II, was the real merry-go-round in his life that would change him forever. This detachment from those close to him, his friends and his new spiritual Family was the test of fire of the Spirit that accompanied his project, amidst his own frailities and strengths.

An Unbelievable Rebirth

In Rome, between June 23 and July 21, 1962, the Minister General of the Franciscans encouraged him to pursue his apostolate. On August 25, 1962, Father Menard founded the Society of the Missionaries of the Holy Apostles (M.SS.A.), which would be considered a Pious Union. He resided in Washington, DC, from 1962 to 1967 within the properties acquired during his first foundation. He lived in Peru from 1967 to 1987.

Aided by his Canadian and American confreres and supported by bishops like Bishop Laberge and Bishop Guibord, from the Apostolic Vicariate of San José Del Amazonas, many apostolates saw the day: a Seminary (Ricardo Palma 1964), a Retreat Centre (Chacrasana 1973), a residence "La Semilla" (Chosica 1977), a hospital "Hogar San Pedro" (Ricardo Palma 1979), Hogar San Juan (Lima 1981).... Father Menard accepted the Sanctuary of the Blessed Trinity (Lima 1979) and acquired Winnetka College (Chaclacayo 1980). Sisters Rosa Huaman and Zelmina Torres joined him in 1981 and founded the Fraternity of the Missionary Sisters of the Holy Apostles of Peru. Moreover, other confreres founded the MSA Seminary of Bogota (Colombia 1966).

While Father Menard was Episcopal Vicar of the province of Huarichiri (1967/1976) and of the province of Cajatambo (1977/1982) Peru, confreres were working in parishes in Ricardo Palma (Peru 1967) and Campinas (Brazil 1967). On the other hand, the Society of the Holy Apostles in Canada opened the Seminary of the Holy Apostles in Nsimalen, in the diocese of Yaoundé (Cameroon 1966), transferred in 1968 to Otélé.

While in Africa, Father Menard stopped in Cameroon from May 30 to June 2, 1978 to visit his confreres and Bishop Zoa, Archbishop of Yaoundé. This visit became an historic moment of reconciliation between Father Menard and Cardinal Leger who resided in a parish with Father Pierre-Julien Bouchard. How could two men who preached the Gospel so effectively not be reconciled someday?

In 1985, initiated by Father Roland Barrette (1938–2006) began a pastoral presence of MSA at the Monastery of the Poor Clares (French) of Assisi, Italy. From 1986 to 1998, the Holy Apostles took on the direction of the Seminary of Saint-Paul in Bangui (Central African Republic).

A Few More Significant Aspects

Father Menard was a happy priest, some-times tormented, always fascinated by God's wonderful plan for humanity in the Word of

God. A listener and a comforter, he contemplated divine love in people he met. An apostle of the Eucharist, he placed his priestly ministry in the hands of Mary, Queen of the Apostles and the apostles of yesterday and today, witnesses of Christ who inspired his preaching, his texts and conferences.

A man of prayer, faithful to his daily meditation, passionate, daring, creative, Father Menard was not a gifted writer, but a preacher on fire. *I cannot live outside a retreat house. I need it so much for myself!* (CF 83) A convincing apostle, he brought together Church documents and writings of various authors who *are able to put at our disposal, in a language adapted to our times, the richness of faith that never changes: the Just man lives by faith* (Rm 1:17/RV2, p. III). This is one of his strengths. The spirituality of Father Menard is not found in what he may have written, but in the Gospel, the life of Jesus and of the first Christians.

Father Menard is one of the Lord's instruments sent to the world at a precise historic moment for the good of the Church whom he loved with all his soul, with all his heart, with all his being even in difficult times. Attentive to the Holy Spirit, he dared to undertake new roads because of the needs of the Church and of the world.

The Apostolate Continues

Having passed away in Montreal on March 26, 1987 following a trying illness, Father Menard invites us with our talents, our human frailties, to be salt of the earth and light of the world for each one of us, *we are instruments in a universal symphony that is beyond us and submerges us. A Christian is someone to whom Jesus Christ has entrusted all humankind. Nothing that concerns the interest of a single person can be foreign to him* (TS, p. 74).

Providence continues the apostolate with the creation of the Institute of Philosophy Saint-Joseph Mukasa in partnership with three religious congregations (Cameroon 1989); the foundation of homes in Los Teques (Venezuela 1989), Nkolo-Bisson (1991) and Fëbë (2003) in Cameroon as well as parishes in Colombia (1993), Venezuela (1994) Cameroon (1995, 2002, 2009) and Peru (2010). In 1991, the laity in Europe came together with Mr. Bernard Prouvost of Antibes (France).

On August 15, 1995, Cardinal Jean-Claude Turcotte, Archbishop of Montreal, proclaimed the decree of erection of the new Society of the Missionaries of the Holy Apostles (MSA) during the General Assembly for the union between the S.SS.A. and the M.SS.A., so greatly desired by Father Menard. The mission continues: to promote, form and accompany young people and adults in their vocation to the priestly ministry and to other ministries in the Church (CN #1). As of today, more than one thousand priests ordained for the Church have come from MSA houses of formation.

Father Menard burning with love for the Lord lived his fruitful vocation within a spirituality of Pentecost in an ambience of Magnificat. Just as Christ sent his apostles on a mission, Father Menard is on a persevering crest, strong and brilliant as a diamond of many facets. Nothing can stop him. Thanks to his contagious dynamism, he continues to send us to the heart of the world which, more than ever, needs to know Jesus: *Broaden your outlook and heart; extend them to all countries and to all peoples* (RF, p. 15).

On the Threshold of
This Spiritual Encounter ...

Dear Father Menard,

It is on a Sunday, 6 of January 1985, in Paris, in the entrance hall of the *Frères de Jérusalem* (Brothers of Jerusalem), that I learned of the existence and history of your numerous foundations thanks to Father Yves Bégin, M.S.A. Though I never met you, I was struck by your audacity and prophetic courage. *Do you know how we begin an apostolate? It is when we have nothing and depend on others and keep almost nothing for ourselves. The more we receive, the less do we keep for ourselves* (CF 78). The diversity of charisms, apostolates and journeys of the members of this Society of Apostolic Life, presently of Pontifical Right, awakened my interest to the point of entering in November 1989 and being ordained a priest in 1995.

This apostolate initiated, thanks to a profound wide vision containing universal perspectives, has grown beyond Quebec bearing fruit as far as South America, Africa, the United States and Europe.

A man full of projects … *The projects of the Lord are always wonderful projects* (CF 78)*!* You had moments. like other founders did in the history of the Church, of joy, of tribulations, that come with maturing and development.

During your entire life, you held the course of maintaining confidence in Divine Providence never backing off in front of difficulties or new challenges. Your belief was that wherever there was a need, we must take the first steps and God does the rest. You even wrote on the walls of your seminaries this illustrious saying: "What I know of tomorrow is that Providence will rise before the sun!"

Son of Francis of Assisi, friend of the poor, the afflicted, the abandoned, to humanize and evangelize are the two inseparable roads of your life. You have the audacity, even after your death, to continue spurring us on because *for us, Christians of today, this means that we must work , each and everyone, at replacing our old hearts bored by the daily routines with young hearts that want to beat at the rhythm of the Gospel and of the Council* (TS, p. 55).

Dear Father Menard, you could have been the author of these pages. Besides, they are filled with your words. During these fifteen days, readers will discover and others will rediscover a few of the principal themes of the spirituality that you transmitted with enthusiasm to your

M.S.A. brothers and sisters as well as to many lay friends working for the Church. Help us remember that it is in progressing yonder as Jesus would say to Peter, at the heart of the realities of this world, where storms are raging, that each baptized person will recognize his (her) vocation and mission in the footsteps of Christ. May your prayer be answered for all of us: *Lord, render our hearts human enough so that when our brothers enter them, they may feel at home* (BF, Summer 2002)*!*

Your spiritual son

Abbreviations

Works and documents:

AGF   Assemblée générale de la Fondation Père Ménard

APM   Allocution du Père Ménard (8 avril 1956)

AS   De l'atelier au Séminaire (1956)

ATH   À toute heure, à tout âge (1968)

BC   Bulletin et Communiqué/Ensemble (1987–1998)

BF   Bulletin de la Fondation Père Ménard

BLA   Bulletin of Lay Associates (1964)

CF   Conférences annuelles de la Fondation Père Ménard (1978–1985)

CN   Constitutions and Norms (2006)

CSA   Cette soif d'aimer (1984)

CVII   Council Vatican II

CVS   Consignes de vie spirituelle (1960 – 1962)

DRC   Émission "Dialogue" du 5 mai 1981, Radio Canada

DSPV   Donnons un sens positif à notre vie (1986)

ETQA   L'église telle que je l'aime (1983)

HOM1 Homélie du 29 janvier 1981

HOM2 Homélie du 25 mai 1981

INT   Entrevue au Journal « L'Informateur Catholique», Fondation Père Ménard (1982)

ITP   Il faut toujours prier

LF   Le Filet

LPL   Lettres au père Marc Lussier (1987)

LRA   La révolution de l'amour (1985)

MN   Messages de Noël (1960 ; 1967)

MP   Message de Pâques (1960)

OVE   Orientaciones para vivir conforme al Evangelio

PVH   Pour vivre heureux (1982)

QAM   Quelques attitudes d'un Missionnaire des Saints-Apôtres (1975)

RAD   Émissions à la Radio (1956)

RES   Résolutions (1940)

RF   Réflexions

RRS   Renouvellement intérieur et réconcilia-tion par l'intermédiaire du Sacré-Coeur

RS   Retraite spirituelle (non publié)

RV1   Règle de Vie: texte d'introduction (FR) (1989)

RV2   Règle de Vie (FR) (1989)

TS   Spiritual Testament (2006)

URV   Una regla de vida (1997)

VN   Vœux de Noël aux confrères en Afrique (1977)

1
Son of Francis of Assisi

Focus Point

////////////

The world is in a constant state of transformation. Technological changes progress at a lightning speed. Peoples, cultures and languages merge. Moral standards evolve. The economic and political systems of the world have become the driver of the globalization of our planet. What a challenge for the upcoming generations! St. Francis of Assisi and Father Menard, two witnesses to Christ, each living his commitment at different times in history, challenge us to live each day rooted in God.

////////////

Let's begin with a profound conviction that charity will someday conquer violence, selfishness and money. We belong to Christ only when we belong to others. Our way of dealing with our neighbor is a faithful mirror of

our attitude towards God. Do not scorn your
brother because he is of a different race, for
we all belong to the same race, that of God. It
is not sufficient to love others, we must show
it. You are distributors of God's gifts and not
their owner (AGF 78).

*F*rancis of Assisi lived from 1182–1226.
At the time of the Crusades, the West
experienced an economic, spiritual and cultural
upheaval. The Catholic Church, during this
time, with the Fourth Council of Lateran (1215)
convoked by Innocent III, went through a
flourishing and influential time. The Franciscans
lived close to the people, in the heart of the cities,
giving time to prayer, preaching and helping
the poor. Francis encouraged his brothers to
live simply and humbly by remaining close to
the underprivileged, so much so that the first
brothers refused to own any property whether
private or communal.

Francis, mendicant of the Gospel, artisan of
peace, servant of the poor, missionary pilgrim,
universal brother of creation, companion of
joy, master-builder, worshipper of the Eucharist
showed great respect and reverence for the
priesthood. How can we not find a spiritual
and filial connection between Father Menard
and Saint Francis?

In 1946, Father Menard founded his Apostolate in Montreal. Emerging from World War ll,

the West was undergoing a profound reformation. Political alliances from East and West made their mark. In 1960, in the province of Quebec, "The Quiet Revolution" began. This was a time of deep rooted change in the Quebec society with laicism challenging the family and the Church, its two traditional pillars: a diminishing in the number of children per couple, a sexual revolution, a progressive lowering of religious practice, an increase in the divorce rate …

Among others, profound changes took place in the area of education, in the medical sector and social services, until then principally under the direction of the Church. Furthermore, the "Belle Province" experienced a "renewal of Quebec nationalism" on the cultural as well as the political and economic level. From 1962 to 1965, the Church lived a historic moment with the arrival of the Second Vatican Council convoked by Blessed John XXIII calling for an "aggiornamento." In 1968, France and the United States witnessed the uprising of huge student demonstrations. The feminist movement was revived.

Father Menard, a Franciscan in sandals, identified himself with *François d'Assise, mon frère (Francis of Assisi, my brother)* (TS, p. 26). Francis' life is more entrenched in the heart of God than in doctrine. Like Francis, *a man of the Gospel* (RV2, p. 83), Father Menard is captivated by the Good News and lived it fully by following Christ, poor — *the living rule of Francis* (RV2, p. 283) — with a special love for the little ones and the underprivileged. *Thank you, Francis of Assisi, for being poor and for your great inspiration* (TS, p. 8; RS #50). God knows how much he modeled Francis! Doesn't the Rule of life of the Franciscans tell us to live the Gospel by following Christ?

An untiring preacher, ardent witness of the Word of God, always on the lookout for young adults seeking to commit themselves to work for the Church and in the world, Father Menard was a pilgrim builder who, journeying from place to place, founded several seminaries, works of charity and retreat houses. At all times he encouraged a fraternal lifestyle, living an unconditional welcome to each and everyone, especially priests with difficulties in their personal lives or priestly ministry. He recognized Jesus, without hesitation, in each one of them.

In the framework of formation for seminarians, he prescribed work among the sick: give them baths and clean their rooms like Francis who formed his first disciples, not with a series of conferences but by practical and charitable actions. *The poor teach us what we don't find in books. We are the voice of those who have no voice, the hand of those who have no hands, the bridge between the haves and the have-nots* (RV1, p. 6).

He found nourishment in contemplation and the wonderment of God's love and hoped to live the perfect joy like Francis did: *Thanks for allowing me to taste the perfect joy that Francis of Assisi so well described: it is the most beautiful commentary of the Beatitudes I have ever encountered* (TS, p. 37). Not experiencing it every day, he, later wrote: *How I desire to taste the perfect joy that Francis describes* (TS, p. 70). His life as an apostle is marked by the "humble prayer" attributed to Francis of Assisi that invites us to meditate for this is where we find *the answer to many problems in community and apostolic life. It will help you live the reality of daily living your spirituality of the Mystical Body of Christ* (TS, p. 17): "Lord, make me an instrument of your peace. Where there is hatred, let me sow love …"

In 1985, Father Menard was diagnosed with an incurable disease. He lived it like Francis in total communion with Christ. On January 6, 1986, his 70th birthday, a good time to revise his long and rich life journey, he recalled Francis reflecting in his innermost being how *a man is worth what he is worth in the eyes of God and nothing more* (TS, p. 72). All for the glory of God (RS #37) and nothing for the glory of man (RS #38). He then asked God *a great favor: with the strength of your Spirit, I want to put into practice these instructions:* "To carry one another's burdens; thus, you shall have accomplished the Law of Christ (Ga 6:2)" (TS, p. 74).

In 1981, he wrote concerning the saints who accomplished *frightening ascetical practices,* that Francis, towards the end of his life, asked forgiveness of his brother mule, his body, for the excesses he committed. He added: *And he was right* (TS, p. 52). Father Menard also, from time to time, had to ask forgiveness to brother mule, his body, for the rhythm of life he demanded during his long priestly ministry. He advised his brothers: "As each one has received a gift, use it to serve one another as good stewards of God's varied grace" (1 P 4:10).

I accept my death …
And I want it to be a prayer …
I believe, Lord Jesus, in eternal life.
I want my death to be an act of faith in
your omnipotence
That crushes me in order to resurrect me,
In your mercy that showers me and
breathes new life into me,
In your gracious goodness that takes
everything away so as to fulfill me.
I accept my death …
To thank you for your goodness,
For I have nothing but what your goodness
has given me.
You can have it all back, O my God,
Whenever you want and however you want it.

I want my death to be a way of saying
thank you
And to proclaim that I depend entirely on
you.
I accept my death!
May my last breath be an act of love!

(TS 24–25)

Reflection Questions

Today, which attribute of St. Francis of Assisi's life touches you in a special way? In the eyes of God, each human being is unique. How do I receive my brothers and sisters of the human family who seem so different and yet who belong to the same human race as I do... God's race?

2
To Give Leaders to the Church

Focus Point

////////////

Through the ages, the place and role of the Church in society has evolved. Today, in many countries, religion is relegated to the private sphere of life. Pope Benedict XVI speaks of a Christianity of choice. Yet, human beings have always sought out eloquent eyewitnesses to Love in the world. The harvest is abundant. The workers are few. Our Lord continues to call believers to follow Him ...

////////////

Priests and Laity

Give me a priest who possesses the honesty of an ambassador, the tenderness of a father and the concern of a shepherd, the courage of a leader who carries the cross, the prudence of a sovereign and the watchful eye of a caretaker, the skill of a pilot at the helm, the patience of a fisherman and the endurance of a laborer, the consummate art of a guide, the divine inspiration of a prophet, the science of a master and the Love of a Savior (AS, p. 99)*!*

*F*ather Menard believed that there was not a shortage of priestly vocations in the Church, for the Holy Spirit is present to the world. He invited each Christian to be attentive. *At any time, at any age, Christ can invite us to follow Him. God chooses whoever he wants* (ATH, pp. 96–97). *It is not age, but souls that God calls* (AS, p. 27). "Consider your own calling, brothers. Not many of you were wise by human standards, … not many were of noble birth. Rather, God chose the foolish of the world to shame the wise …" (1 Co 1:26–31). His wisdom surpasses all human wisdom.

Knowing the world greatly needs spiritual guides, he lent a special attention to young adults who, tomorrow, would be able to assume this task. The term adult *must be understood not only in the sense of age, but in a special way, in the sense of human and spiritual maturity in Christ* (RV 1, p. 6/Ep. 4:11–16). He reminded us that *Jesus founded his Church with mature men and young people who had a trade and were passionately interested in the great social, political and religious problems of their country and of their time* (ATH, p. 95).

In his travels throughout the world, he was surprised to find that what the Church lacked most acutely was an attentive fostering of vocations, faith educators, witnesses who dared uphold the greatness and joy of being a priest and the pride of being a Christian. *It is urgent, essential, for modern man to rediscover Christ. Leading him to this encounter is an immense task* (BF 75) and it necessitates happy witnesses. In 1967, he wrote in signing a book that *in spite of difficulties and dark days built into any life, I have never regretted one day spent as a priest* (ATH, p. 139).

For each generation, the Church needs men and women who can awaken in the heart of young adults the desire to become priests or Christian leaders in the world. The MSA helps this ecclesial service where there is a need for priests and apostolic laborers. They establish centers for the promotion, formation and accompaniment of vocations or collaborate with similar institutions. They establish centers for the proclamation of the Word of God or collaborate with them. They always bear in mind the establishment and growth of the Kingdom of God (CN #3, 4 and 13).

Father Menard appreciated the marvels that the Holy Spirit accomplishes in each person for through each priest and Christian layperson, it is this echoing voice of Christ that continues to reach cities and the countrysides proclaiming the law of Love, the Beatitudes.

It is urgent for our world that humanity be revitalized in the waters of baptism. It is a challenging task. It is about carrying the needs of human life along with its difficulties, its burdens of conscience, its temptations, its commitments, its different situations to the Eucharist in order to penetrate the mentality of humankind and the structures of society with the Gospel (ATH, pp. 26/84). It is a challenge that remains most relevant for the actual Church.

Today as yesterday, young people need beacons, headlights, examples like: the curé of Ars "the holy patron of all priests of the universe" who used to say that only in eternity will we understand the greatness of the priest; devoted priests of our parishes; committed laypersons, anonymous or known, like Jean Vanier, Chiara Lubich, Catherine de Hueck-Doherty, Dorothy Day ... who are a living witness of faith and hope.

Firstly, Father Menard considered Saint John the Baptist, the Precursor (Mt 11:11; Lk 1:13–17) as *an incomparable model of virtues necessary for priests and future priests, particularly humility, mortification, strength and renunciation.... May he become the model of those who have the formidable responsibility among others, of forming for their future mission candidates to the priesthood ... may he help our common efforts through his power-*

ful intercession, and obtain for us in abundance the blessings of Him who gives us growth and prosperity (AS, pp. 46–49).

Father Menard believed that, in spite of the crisis the Church is experiencing, vocations exist in great numbers. The hearts must simply be cleared like the first monks cleared the forests to construct their abbeys. Just as Jesus underwent the temptations in the desert, young adults undergo temptations of their time: individualism, relativism, and laxism. It was essential for him to repeat the call of the Master of the harvest with the same words and the strength of the Spirit. Young adults are absolute and generous, maybe more so than in the past. They are looking for happiness and wish to give their lives for those they love. Requiring a quality of life, enriched by their desires and aspirations, are we able to receive them? Are we capable of accompanying them, that is, journeying with them like Christ walked side by side with the disciples of Emmaus?

This mad desire to give priests and committed laypersons in the service of God and of the world is deeply rooted in our hearts. With this enthusiasm that characterized him so well, does he not exclaim that the Church has a great need for priests, men of the Gospel, of the Eucharist and of a praying Assembly, convinced, joyful, happy, *priests who do not repeat what others have*

*prepared but give an experience of a life, a relation-
ship with the Lord , who cry out with all their might
and the actions of their lives, the wonder of being a
Christian, the joy of being a priest* (CF 78)*!*

Father Menard saw many young adults
take the road of the priesthood without having
given it much thought. They chose it because
one day they met a witness of the living Christ
who dared speak in His name. To dare speak!
To dare look as Christ did to those he called to
be his first disciples: "Come follow me, and I
will make you fishers of men" (Mk 1:17). It is
our turn to challenge others, for in any being,
whatever his cultural origin, social condition,
strengths or weaknesses may be, even in the
most obscure circumstances of his existence,
God can shower upon him the marvels of His
grace. *Happy is he who has this sickness of the
priesthood and is able to become contagious* (CS 73)*!*
United beyond boundaries and oceans, in the
spirit of the Gospel, let us pray each day:

Most heavenly Father,
Your Son Jesus said:
*"The harvest is plentiful, but the laborers
few;*
*Pray therefore the master of the harvest to
send laborers to his harvest."*
*We pray to you with confidence according
to the desire of your Heart.*
Give each Christian the awareness of their

responsibility
As citizens of the Kingdom and living rocks
of your Church.
Choose from among your People, apostolic
laborers,
Priests, deacons, religious brothers and
sisters, committed laypersons,
So that the Good News may be proclaimed
to all Nations and
That your mercy be known to all our brothers
and sisters.
Amen.

(MSA prayer for Vocations)

Reflection Questions

At any time, at any age, Christ's call surges out of the nitty-gritty of this world. What is my down-to-earth answer to this invitation? In what ways do I take to discover my talents and develop them to help others and to the telling of the Good News? What do I do to strengthen my faith so as to give a Christian witness around me?

3
All Baptized Christians are Called to Holiness

Focus Point

////////////

"Like-Love". We often use these two words in our everyday conversation, popular songs, poems, literature, TV programs, on the internet … But, how often are they trivialized? How often are they ridiculed in our own everyday relationships? Father Menard, spent his whole life urging his followers to rediscover the real meaning of these words.

////////////

*The greatest force in the world is love. You are capable of loving with the strength of the heart of God. You are the temple of God and it is within you that the most important liturgy for the heavenly Father takes place …
throughout your days as you go about your work…. Be proud of your home. You can*

compare it favourably to all the cathedrals of the world. And, in this home, there is each one of you which is the most beautiful temple because it was built, not by men, but by the most Holy Trinity. Have only one ambition: to be what you are in the role you accomplish in your home. Try to discover the talents that the Lord has given you and use them to the full (CF 85).

*W*ith these powerful words that move our heart, Father Menard was speaking to numerous couples who had founded a family, a patrimony of humanity, on the privileged theme of love and commitment in the specific environment of Christian and family life. For him, *one does not need to be learned, powerful, a hero, a star in order to become a saint* (TS, p. 48).

To fully attain our mission as Christians, Father Menard reminds us that in the tradition of the Gospel, there exists only one perfection that can guide us, Christ himself. Everyone is called to live according to the radicalism of the Gospel, by putting into practice the Beatitudes and by following the advice and example of Christ himself. This is one of the corner stones of his preaching.

God is free with his gifts.... He does not necessarily join his choices and gifts of his graces to our qualities and natural talents (TS, pp. 46–47). He gives each one the necessary graces to attain the ideal of perfection. With baptism, the Christian is called to live his faith with joy and coherence in the world, as a witness to God's infinite tenderness. By the anointing he received, he is part of God's people. He is an eternal member of Jesus Christ, priest, prophet and king.

Father Menard believed that there is but one Christian vocation expressed in different ways, for Jesus associates us to his work of salvation through baptism. With enthusiasm and audacity, all of us, in communion with one another, priests and laity participate in the priesthood of Christ and are co-responsible for the construction of the society according to the Gospel.

To live our baptism is not only to take it seriously, but to live a consecrated life by following Christ, which implies a total and specific commitment to each lifestyle. "There are different kinds of spiritual gifts but the same Spirit; there are different forms of service but the same Lord; there are different workings but the same God who produces all of them in everyone …" (1 Co 12:4–11).

All baptized Christians receive from Christ, as did the Apostles, the order of the mission to be the yeast of God's love. Whether we are a married layperson, celibate, a father, a mother, a religious brother or sister, a company manager, a blue collar worker or a member of the MSA Family, Jesus sends us on a mission: "Go into the whole world and proclaim the gospel to every creature" (Mk 16:15).

For Father Menard, the layperson has never been a second class citizen as a Christian, a believer on sale and lost somewhere in the anonymity of a crowd. "Whoever is a follower of Christ, the perfect man, becomes himself more of a man" (CV II, *Gaudium et Spes* 41:1). The whole Mystical Body of Christ is affected. The call to holiness is common to the whole Church. He is convinced that the greatest failure, the greatest sin on earth is to not develop the talents that God gives abundantly: intellectual, manual, spiritual, financial talents. It is a question of becoming aware of the dignity but also of the responsibility that is ours as Christians seeking to live our mission and to work earnestly to make the world a better place and to allow love to triumph (AS, p. 15). We are called to be disciples and missionaries of Jesus Christ so that our people may have life in Him. Holiness flourishes in each of its members. *It is a great joy for each person to recognize each other as brothers, as sons of the same Father* (RV2, p. IX).

The greatest challenge in Christian life is to accept the free gift of God's infinite love, to taste his peace and his joy, to share these around us. Father Menard states that this is a life or death decision. He invites us to wrap ourselves in the beauty and tenderness of our heavenly Father and to live like the Lord Jesus who spent his life proclaiming the Good News until his death on the cross.

It is an art to learn how to live truthfully with oneself; to discover our qualities and to be conscious of our limitations; to welcome and accept that others are different from ourselves. It is an art to become beautiful with Christ's beauty. The prospects of vocations and the mission of all baptized Christians will appear in a practical and concrete manner to each generation, for God will never manufacture human beings on an assembly line (RS #53–56). Each one is unique in God's heart. He *never scorns the human values within us. Do they not come from him? And if he has made us congenial, or has given us some unpretentious talents, he wants us to develop them* (TS, p. 46).

Relentlessly, Father Menard questioned the purpose of our lives, while reminding us to be aware of the needs of our immediate surroundings. Whoever we may be, whatever our age, how does the Word of God penetrate and fashion our daily living? How can we be most useful on this earth?

With the talents that God gives me, where and how can I best serve my brothers and sisters? And thus be a happier person? How can I better my relationship with God (RV2, p. 226)? *Are you attentive to the signs of the times? Are you passionately involved with your times? Are you attentive to the signs, the direction of God's action, the callings and inspirations of the Spirit? Have you discovered in your life something good enough to want to be a part of it forever* (LRA, pp. 29–30)? *Do you love your life? Do you believe in your work? Do you have respect and love for your existence* (LRA, p. 37)?

Father Menard considered that our mission cannot be reduced to only a few social and political activities. For him, it is the whole family life, of couples, of work at different levels, national, international, economic and political, that we must update, construct, renovate in Christ. Only then will there be a better world, a more just and free, more united and authentic world where love replaces hate, compassion replaces cruelty (RRS, p. 2). *The whole of humanity needs you, wherever you happen to be, unique and, therefore, irreplaceable. What are you waiting for* (RV2, p. 226)?

My wish:
In contemplating the heart of Jesus,
May we all experience
That the greatest joy in the world is to serve,
That the greatest strength in the world is
to love
And the greatest victory in the world
Is to have conquered oneself.

(RRS, p. 6)

Reflection Questions

Am I mindful that I, too, am called to holiness each day and that this means since my baptism? Father Menard offers several focus points for our reflection in this discerning of our life choices. I follow them, as a kind of spiritual retreat, to find out where I am in answering the call of the Lord, in the here and now.

4
Laity and Priests: Together

Focus Point ////////////

At the very beginning of his public life, Jesus chose 12 Apostles. 72 disciples joined them. The first Christian communities were formed, eventually. The Acts of the Apostles offers an account of this. During his life, Father Menard carried a deep conviction in his heart, that the priest and laypeople hand-in-hand as a team, is absolutely essential to the spreading of the Gospel.

////////////

We want ... God to be better known and better loved in the world ... that men take advantage of the redemptive work of Christ, seeking, before anything else, the Glory of God and this is the reason for our consecration.... To love God because it is He who created us out of love and because so many forget the Lord, our love must be one

Laity and Priests: Together   45

*of gratitude. And we do not forget that this
God of love sent us his Son out of love for
us, and the Son reveals the love of the Father
for us and his love for the Father* (MN 60).

*F*rom the very beginning, Father Menard
was convinced that the work of the Holy
Apostles is a work of God. *It is not my work.
You kept me, O Jesus, from any illusions: it is your
work, O Jesus. Do not forget, Lord, that this Society
is your little flock. It is yours. It is your work and not
the work of Father Menard* ... (TS, pp. 36/70). It
began with a great respect and a great love for
the royal priesthood of Christ Jesus in which all
of us participate through our baptism.

The spirituality of the MSA and the crucial
place given to the laity at the outset of its foundation take root in two Biblical texts in Saint
Paul that we must read and meditate: *"For
through faith you are all children of God in Christ
Jesus. For all of you who were baptized into Christ
have clothed yourselves with Christ. There is neither
Jew nor Greek ... for you are all one in Christ Jesus.
And if you belong to Christ, then you are Abraham's
descendant, heirs according to the promise"* (Ga
3:26–29). *"Stop lying to one another, since you have
taken off the old self ... and have put on the new
self, which is being renewed, for knowledge, in the
image of its creator; Here there is not ... slave, free,
but Christ is all and in all"* (Col 3:9–11).

Father Menard sought to rediscover the spirit of the first Christians in his foundation reminding us that *during the first centuries of the Church, faith was spread thanks to the enthusiastic collaboration of the laity and the Apostles and that from the ranks of these laypersons came most of the martyrs* (BLA).

In the ecclesial thinking of his time, the founding charism of Father Menard was, to say the least, original and daring. One of the characteristics of his apostolate was to gather priests and laity, together, for the humanization and evangelization of the world, each according to one's talents and duties, counting especially on the Holy Spirit, the soul of the apostolate and prayer. He was convinced that to attain this pastoral objective, laity and priests must lead an intense spiritual life. For him, the degree of one's union with God determines the apostolic productivity. *May they not forget at all times that their objective is most crucial for the whole human family.... May they not hesitate to pay the price. What was so costly for Jesus cannot be acquired cheaply by them* (TS, p. 16).

In all his activities, he promoted the integration of laity for each one has a proper task to accomplish. He is accompanied by men and women rooted in their faith and seeking to work in the vineyard of the Lord. The world needs apostles capable of bringing to their brothers and sisters the explosive force of the Gospel. *He who collaborates with the Apostle will receive the reward of the Apostle* (LF, March 1992). *Committed laypersons are co-responsible for our works. Laypersons who can think, laypersons who are creative, laypersons who assist us and support our hand,* he used to say, as he invited the Church on these occaions to rid herself of a mentality that was too clerical.

This unique intuition, precursor and pro-phetic, prefigures the very clear teaching received at the Second Vatican Council. The laity will be recognized as witnesses and living instruments of the Church's mission, mea-sured by the gift of Christ. They see themselves given a particular role in the world and in the midst of these different economic, social and political realities, as well as a specific mission to assume responsibilities and to live accord-ing to the Spirit of the Word of God (CV II, *Lumen Gentium* #31/32). Yet there remains a reluctance to collaborate actively with the laity in the Church. But for Father Menard, there was absolutely no doubt: *the hand that supports the priest supports the world* (CF 78/AGF 84)*!*

Concerning this, it is appropriate to remind ourselves of the words of Cardinal Leger pronounced on November 24, 1969, to the numerous benefactors and members of the Society, seven years after the events of 1962; "If the Holy Apostles exercise a spiritual ministry that is quite particular, it is because they are the first to have succeeded before the Council in putting into practice what the Council asked us to do, that is, to invite the laity to participate more fully in the works of the Church."

How many times did Father Menard say that without the collaboration of the laity, the Work of the Holy Apostles would not exist? This is why he is a pioneer in the church of the twentieth century creating a stronger awareness of the layperson's responsibility in the communion and mission of the Church.

This precious and indispensable collaboration of the laity allows the priests to give themselves entirely to their priestly ministry in the world and *to give themselves more totally to prayer and to the Word of God* (RV1, p. 4) like the Apostles (Ac 6:4). *May they live their priesthood in union with that of their baptized brothers, giving the latter many responsibilities so that they themselves are able to dedicate themselves to prayer and to preaching the word* (TS, p. 11).

Father Menard believed that the revolution of love cannot take place without the collaboration of committed laypersons (LRA, p. 3). The Church absolutely needs enterprising and responsible laypersons who will build the Kingdom of God using their imagination and radiating an apostolic zeal that overflows with life and a rejuvenating spirit. And if, at times, they feel surpassed by the extent of the task, *let them remind themselves that they are only instruments in the hands of God and that it is He alone who accomplishes the good* (BLA).

Jesus,
I thank you
And I wish to thank you
Each moment of my life
And during all of eternity
Because you love us
With a gratuitous love:
An unconditional love,

A love that is for everyone
Indistinctly,
A love that loves us
Without merit and without virtue.
We are so poor
That we are unable to love you
But with the love you have taught and
given us.

…
Such is the profession of faith
That is required of me
During my entire life
And at the moment of my death.

(TS, p. 42)

Reflection Questions

In my parish, in my daily comings-and-goings, what do I do to foster a spirit of fraternal collaboration? Do I share this part of my life with the other Christians around me? What can we change to better contribute to the mission as a whole? Do I take the time to re-read and meditate on the Acts of the Apostles so as to revitalize the energies of the fraternal life of this team; priests and laypeople working together in mission?

5
The Wonderful
Plan of God

Focus Point

////////////

How many times have we heard that what is wrong with family life, with the life of a couple, with the world in general, with Christian communities, with a fraternity, with a monastery … is due to the "other" who refuses to change! Now, what if each one of us took time out to meet the "other", sat down with them, listened to them, let them talk about what really makes them tick!

////////////

One of the secrets of happiness is to be able to put up with ourselves and our neighbor. He who does not accept himself as he is in order to improve himself, is at risk of not being able to improve at all (CVS 21, July 1960). The battlefield is within us! It is there that we fight

our most alarming battles! If, as far as our
intentions are concerned, we do not set limits
to our desires of perfection, we must, actually,
face our sins, our desires, our limitations, our
concupiscence (RV2, p. 108).

*G*od sows in each human being, in the most
intimate part of his heart, a desire to be
loved, to be truthful and to become a saint. The
depth and scope of this divine project are not easy
to discover in our present world. The challenges
are great. Father Menard identifies four of them.

The first challenge consists in simply
accepting this admirable project of God's
love for us: "love one another as I have loved
you" (Jn 15:12). The second challenge is to
take the necessary time to become familiar,
each one according to his ability, with God's
plan. The third challenge is to share it humbly
according to our talents and limitations.
The fourth challenge, and not the least one,
is found in our own human frailty. Father
Menard underlines, that all human beings
are prone to resisting God's marvellous plan
through selfishness. My personal selfishness
… According to him, the greatest victory in
the world will be to conquer my own personal
selfishness.

In order to accept in faith, to understand
and live fully the rich and marvellous plan of

God engraved in the depths of each human being, Father Menard refers us to three Biblical texts that, for him, contain a fundamental and essential teaching, a rock upon which we can lean, where the source of each vocation resides: Jn 15:1–17; Eph 1:3–14 and 1 Co 12:12–31. He studied, meditated and prayed them. At every moment, he sought to be in touch with Christ, the source of life. His ardent desire was to introduce each Christian to discover the depths of divine love. His joy was to know that each baptized Christian is in fervent communion with Christ, expressing an unspeakable beauty.

The words of Saint Paul clearly situate the deep-rootedness of this admirable plan of God for us: "Blessed be the God and Father of our Lord Jesus Christ…. He chose us in him, before the foundation of the world, to be holy and without blemish before him. In love he destined us for adoption to himself through Jesus Christ …" (Eph 1:3–14).

The life unity of all baptized Christians is Jesus, the true vine that unites us to the Father, the vinegrower (Jn 15:1). Baptized in Christ, the Christian puts on Christ and therefore casts off the old man. He is united to Christ like a branch is to the tree. "I am the vine, you are the branches" (Jn 15:5). We are full time members of the Mystical Body of Christ.

As one who is invited to grow in life, it is in the love of God that the Christian is called to grow. Does not the apostle invite each baptized Christian to dwell in Christ, the very key to this unity "Remain in me, as I remain in you" (Jn 15:4). Rich and poor participate as shoots in the construction of this great love project for the world. "Whoever remains in me and I in him will bear much fruit, because without me you can do nothing" (Jn 15:5). To live in such a dynamic context, to take root in love is to be constantly united in the Mystical Body of Christ who is one: "and all the parts of the body, though many, are one body, so also Christ" (1 Co 12:12).

For Father Menard, the mission of Christians takes place among the richness of different languages, cultures, charisms, gifts, vocations; richness of complementarity, of solidarity, of communion and sharing. To live as the Mystical Body of Christ is to recognize daily in each person a master rather than a servant, to be able to accept ourselves just as we are, to spend our energy building rather than criticizing, to forgive as Christ forgave, to live in a spirit of charity, the bond of perfection, the yeast of unity.

With the love of God, the practice of fraternal charity makes up the climate of Family life. We must breathe charity and practice it as naturally as when we breathe. This means that we must live it. There are persons who do not know how to breathe, who do not know how to fill up their lungs, and they have to practice at improving their breathing. It is the same thing when we practice charity (MN 60).

Thanks to this Family spirit, Father Menard conveyed this rich and precious teaching of Jesus: "For in one Spirit we were all baptized into one body.... We were all given to drink of one Spirit ..." (1 Co 12:13). Priests and laypersons, he wanted everyone to understand, that we are not a kind of collection of persons who accidentally happen to be in the same place for some reason or like persons who each morning take the subway or spend the evening in a football stadium. Day after day, all of us, together without exception, are to build the Reign of Love, this admirable divine plan for the world. It is a question of team work.

These three Biblical texts of great importance express clearly that we are truly important, and how we must live and act in the world: as sons and daughters of God. "To those who did accept him, he gave power to become children of God" (Jn:12). We are his disciples, here and now. "By this is my Father glorified, that you bear much fruit and become my disciples" (Jn 15:8).

At the invitation and example of Father Menard, at least once in our life, each Christian should take the time to write, while kneeling, each one of these texts because they speak to us of unity and diversity. Each day, all baptized Christians should have them before their eyes, in their mind and heart for the mission of a Christian is to be like Jesus. For Father Menard, *Christianity is living Christ* (RV2, pp. 44/47). May we, in each ordinary action of our lives, become witnesses of the very dimension of the life of the Risen Christ. Each moment of our lives has therefore a touch of eternity.

The desire he cherishes most is that the Christian community live by the example of the Twelve, of Mary and of the first Christians as an assembly of men and women who were solid, articulate and fraternal (Ac 2:42–47). It will become possible inasmuch as it becomes "ONE" in Jesus Christ and where each member is in mutual communion with one another. Everyone centered on Christ and filled with the Holy Spirit, responsible for one another, Christians edify one another, sharing what they have and what they are (Ac 2:1–4). Thus, they will become true witnesses of the Risen Christ for the total edification of the Mystical Body of Christ and for the salvation of all humanity (Ac 4:32–37).

> *Thank you,*
> *All my brothers,*
> *Because "together"*
> *We form Christ*
> *And depend on one another.*

(TS, p. 8)

Reflection Questions

The battlefield is within each one of us ...
says Father Menard. When was the last time
I stopped and relaxed to take stock of my life,
noting my responsibilities for my own human
growth and spiritual growth? Do I spend this
time discerning what I truly want to change
within me? Do I seek out reconciliation with
a person near to me at work, in my family, in
fraternity...!

6
Rooted in the Word of God

Focus Point

////////////

How often Christians say they do not have time to read the Gospel! Others complain they hear the same texts over and over ... Fortunately, many saints and witnesses to the faith remind us the importance of spending time with the Word because it is alive and it helps us grow, that it is a lighthouse in the night of our humanity.

////////////

We have only one guide: the Gospel.... The contemplation of Christ in all his actions will help each one of us live more and more fully in his spirit.... MSA has but one rule: to live the Gospel, a law discovered by the first disciples living in the company of Jesus.... It is essential to be with Christ, to

*depend entirely on Him and to never doubt
his Word* (OVE, pp. 6–7).

*T*ruly impassioned by the Bible, Father
Menard entreated us to carry the Word
of God in one hand and a newspaper in the
other. At his bedside, there was always a small
radio, for the Word of God enlightens the realities of the world. It nourishes our spirit and
body and works marvels beyond our dreams.
It transforms individuals by the power of the
Holy Spirit and gives a wise answer to what we
are living. *The Gospel will always pulverize preju-
dices and destroy conformity.* (RAD, 4 September).

As a herald of the Word of God, for him,
the only important source is the Bible, the book
of Life and the dialogue between God and his
human family. He found himself in Saint Paul:
"Woe to me if I do not announce the Gospel"
(1 Co 9:16). He constantly carried a copy of the
Gospels, in pocketbook form (LF March 1990),
because in order to grow in perfection, we must
always have our eyes fixed on Jesus (TS, p. 23):
*Lord Jesus, I come to you because you are calling me.
You want to lead me to the Father.... I am looking
for you because you have already found me. My peace
rests in your fidelity* (TS, p. 38).

From an important area of our house or
room, *may Holy Scripture, be on hand to draw each
day, from its readings and meditation, the sublime*

knowledge of Jesus Christ (Ph 3:8/TS, p. 18). In his room, left intact since 1987, in Villa La Paz, next to his bed, are the four important books of Father Menard: the Bible, the Liturgy of the Hours, the documents of Vatican II and the Constitutions and Norms of the MSA Society.

By allowing the Word of God to echo within us, he assured us that it transforms our lives as it changed the lives of the Apostles. God tells us how much he loves us, that He accepts us just as we are with our limitations, our unhappiness, our sins. *I am truly alive only when I allow your son, Jesus, to live within me.... I am myself only when I become him whom you love, Jesus* (TS, p. 39). We cannot prevent God from loving, for God is Love. *Believe in love. Allow yourselves to be loved. Allow yourselves to be transformed by Him. It's so simple. He is at on our doorstep. I love you ...* (CF 80).

Father Menard was aware that Jesus is not known to the world around him and that the true meaning of life was little understood by his contemporaries led astray by all kinds of daily events. They do not take the time to reflect on the real meaning of their lives. *Allow me to remind you once more about the absolute necessity of placing your entire trust in the goodness and power of Divine Providence who, according to the Gospel, looks after each one of us, for our spiritual, intellectual and temporal needs* (LPL, 4 January 1987).

As Saint Paul advises us, we must speak

about Christ "whether it is convenient or incon-venient" (2 Tim 4:2), use the most modern means put at our disposal, so that the world may know the truth about love: writings, the media, the internet, for *the world is hungry for God more than it is hungry for bread* (CF 83).

It is more profitable, according to him, to spend our time contemplating Jesus Christ than lamenting the sins and wretchedness of man-kind. Certainly, there is darkness in the world. Where there is darkness, then we can furnish the light. There is only one man who could say: "I am the light of the world" (Jn 8:12). It is Jesus Christ, God made man, who died and is risen. *To change the hearts through the strength found in the Word of God who is Spirit and Life, is the mission of the spiritual leader, priest or layper-son; it is the mission of the MSA* (RV1, p. 14). To be project managers of this light of love that the world needs so badly.

Read the Gospel attentively. Spend hours and hours with the Gospels. Beg the Holy Spirit to convert us. We are selfish. Change our hearts! Let us use this wonder-ful capacity called love that is God's own capacity: to love humankind. There is room in our heart for the whole human family. He is there (CF 84).

Just before Father Menard died, he confided: *You are aware of the zeal that I have for proclaiming the Word of God, either during retreats, conferences and short writings. I remember that when I was a*

*student in theology, I spent my free time and our three
months of vacation reading books about the Word of
God, and even enrolled in special courses whenever
possible. I could say that the foundation of the Work
of the Holy Apostles did not prevent me from dedi-
cating myself to spreading the Word of God. It was
never a chore for me, but rather a moment of great
satisfaction* (LPL, 23 January 1987).

Father Menard proposed that we receive the
Bible as a love letter from God written especially
for each one of us. To read it, to "chew" it and to
put it into practice. This is how we will discover
and live our life's journey, one of freedom and
of hope, for His Word renews itself each day. He
quotes a verse in Saint John that he finds to be
the most liberating and convincing words he has
ever meditated: "In this is love: not that we have
loved God, but that he loved us and sent his Son
as expiation for our sins" (1 Jn 4:10).

Dare to penetrate it. Allow it to penetrate
us so as to fulfill our vocation engraved by the
Lord in the most intimate part of ourselves, for
*God has proven to us many times that we are very
valuable in his eyes. He has written our name on the
palm of his hand, and his paternal love takes care of
each one of us as if we were all alone in the world*
(LPL, 14 January 1987).

From experience, Father Menard knew that
*the day we decide to live according to the Gospel, we
condemn ourselves to endlessly surpass ourselves! ...*

Each time we look at Jesus, we take a step forward (RAD, 20 August) ... a step forward in the realization of our mission as disciples of the risen Christ. Jesus said to his disciples: Go forth! That is, don't stay put! Today, he sends his priests in the same manner: Go forth as far as possible! He sends all baptized Christians, young or old: Go forth! *Never say: enough, I am going to stop* ... for *each life, as long as it lasts, must bear fruit* (MN 67).

> *Father, Son and Holy Spirit,*
> *Be eternally praised*
> *In all things and in everyone!* ...
>
> *Thank you for the privilege of living,*
> *Suffering, enjoying, dying,*
> *Of being raised and of contemplating.*
> *Thank you for allowing me to experience*
> *My limitations, my total inability*
> *And your almighty love.*
> *Thank you for calling me to the priesthood*
> *To render the greatest service:*
> *The Eucharist* ...
> *The unique sacrifice of Christ made present*
> *on the altar* ...
> *The immense love of God for man,*
> *The immense love of man for God,*
> *The infallible success of all creation* ...
> *Amen.*

(TS, pp. 7–9)

Reflection Questions

In my apartment, in my home, in my office, in my room, is there a special place for the Word of God, for the Bible? Living the Gospel of Christ is the life challenge for every baptized person. What place does the Word of God have in my daily schedule? How can I organize my day so as to give more time to God and become more sensitized to his Love?

7
Faithful to Mental Prayer

Focus Point

///////////////

When out in the everyday world, it is often difficult for many of us to be silent, to stop and col-
lect ourselves and pray. What good reasons we
offer for putting off that time needed for a quick
prayer and meditation! Yet, we meet God at the
very heart of prayer. Even at the core of the most
hectic city of the world, one can live rooted in
the heart of God, if one chooses to do so!

///////////////

*In prayer and contemplation, man discov-
ers the sense of God, the sense of Christ,
the sense of the Church, the sense of the
other, the sense of creation, the sense of
life.... He who knows prayer knows life.
Everyone who enters within himself finds*

God. Contemplation is to the soul what sleep is to the body: he is rested and reemerged in himself. Apostolate is not about running after souls, but about being the ones that souls run after (Letter to a monk).

*J*esus told his disciples "a parable about the necessity of always praying without becoming weary" (Lk 18:1). In an introductory text on the spirituality of the Sisters of the Holy Apostles, Father Menard presented and developed three traditional moments of Christian prayer: To pray is to be replenished with God. To pray is to live in God. To pray is to rejoice in God (ITP).

Father Menard aspired to be *simply a priest completely absorbed in prayer and by the Word of God.* It is essential to the vocation of the priest for *prayer is the greatest power on earth* (CF 80). *Be faithful to the spirit of mental prayer, to mental prayer itself, to which everything else is subordinated: as is your mental prayer, such is your life, such is your apostolate* (TS, p. 17–18). *When a priest prays, the whole human family is praying* (CF 81). Prayer is the most important mission of all baptized Christians and the most extraordinary form of energy of our lives as followers of Jesus. To pray is to simply engage in an intimate conversation with God (RS 81–84). "Ask and it will be given to you; seek and you will find; knock and the door will be opened to you" (Mt 7:7–11).

The 3rd General Conference of the Latino-American Episcopacy of Puebla greatly highlighted the ministry and spirituality of Father Menard in South America. "A time in real adoration has more value and spiritual impact than the most intense activity, even if it is an apostolic activity (#529)." He asserted that a priest given to at least one hour of mental prayer each day will become an apostle on fire for he will be filled with divine love. *If we want to give Christ to others, let us enjoy being in His presence, and let us become attached to Him. Let us develop within us a taste for heart-to-heart talks with Him* (BC, Letter of 30 July 1961).

As an inheritor of tradition and a faithful witness to mental prayer, Father Menard suggested these daily spiritual exercises: the celebration of the Eucharist; the liturgy of the hours (breviary); an hour of mental prayer imbued with the spirit of Jesus to become more and more a living member of his Mystical Body; spiritual reading of the Bible, especially of the Gospels (minimum 15 minutes); personal reflection on our human frailties in order to deal with our dominant fault of selfishness; a visit to the Blessed Sacrament to thank God for the gift of the Eucharist and the priesthood, and time with Mary praying and meditating the rosary, real life or the Franciscan Crown.

On a road in Latin America, Father Menard met a truck driver. During the trip, this man who he did not know shared with him how much he loved his wife, his children and his work.... Later on, he told us that this truck driver taught him what living prayer is. *This is how to love God! This is how to live in God! The invisible God is present in this woman, these children, who are at the center of this man's work. He is probably a contemplative without knowing it* (CF 85)!

In a practical, concrete manner, daily living nourished the daily prayer of Father Menard. *I read the newspapers. I listen to the news. The problems of the world are our own problems. When we read the newspapers, it is about us, it is our own life we are reading about. This becomes the subject of our prayer and of our efforts.* He prayed about life rather than reciting formulas, useful and precious though they may be, for moments of aridity in our spiritual life. But, in order to pray about life, we must discover how our brothers and sisters live. *We must feel what they feel, share their joys and become one with their sorrows and problems* (CF 82).

Father Menard pointed out a few customary practices of the Church to keep us rooted in a one to one relationship with God: To live our day with a spiritual intention in mind and our eyes focused on Jesus and Mary, without comparing ourselves to others. To accept to work in any area in a prompt and joyful spirit of obedience. Each day accomplish positive acts of charity for our neighbors. Not to judge. Allow God to be responsible for actions and intentions of others. Learn how to hold our tongue. Give ourselves moments of silence each day. Put up with ourselves and with others. Completely avoid complaining and criticizing inwardly or exteriorly. Learn how to smile. Never dramatize events.

The strength of Father Menard's spirituality resides in the desire to place his entire life under the sign of joy, in an atmosphere of the Magnificat. He finds the never-ending source of life and hope in the Beatitudes (RS #95–107/ DSPV, pp. 51–60): "Be joyful and rejoice!... In Jesus who is poor, the Kingdom of Heaven is theirs. In Jesus who is meek and humble, they will inherit the land. In Jesus who mourns, they will be comforted. In Jesus hungry and thirsting, they will be satisfied. In Jesus merciful and the peacemaker, they will be shown mercy and will be called children of God. In Jesus clean of heart, model of purity, they will see God. In Jesus persecuted, theirs is the kingdom of heaven (Mt 5:1–11). On this road of the Beatitudes, Father Menard revealed to us, by every means put at his disposal, the marvels of God and the richness of the Gospel's message,

God is with us every moment of our lives (CF 80). All daily tasks become prayer. This appealing

liturgy to our heavenly Father unfolds throughout our days. Though it is good and enjoyable
to come together to pray and celebrate, *what the
Lord asks each Christian, each priest is to leave the
material temple, the church structure, to enter the real
temple that the home, the family, daily life represents*
(CF 85). This is where Father Menard learned
how to know Jesus Christ more. Digging a well,
receiving a leper from Lima, an abandoned
child … in contact with human misery, he lives
in the heart of God and is in touch with the
true meaning of the Gospel. Life is not something we learn in books only but by praying and
living with those who suffer. *I have so much to
learn from the poor. They have so much to tell me
about the meaning of life, the meaning of things that
last, so that we do not fall into an illusion other than
this peace and this joy that come from Jesus and can
satisfy us* (CF 79).

Thank you Jesus for the Holy Apostles
Oasis
Of Ricardo Palma.
Thank you for all these flowers,
This water so pure,
These varieties of plants of all kinds,
This vegetation so rich,
These animals that are growing
And preparing to become food,
This fresh air,
This sun that is so warm…

Everything reminds us of God
And invites us to give thanks.

…

(TS, p. 64)

Reflection Questions

He who knows how to pray, knows how to live … Does my prayer energize me? When and how much time do I give to daily prayer? Do I develop different aspects of praying both personally and in community: bidding prayers, meditation, spiritual reading, praying the psalms, meditated reading of the Scriptures…?

8
The Eucharist,
His Whole Life

Focus Point

////////////

One of the most intense moments we can spend with God happens at the celebration of the Eucharist. The Eucharist, an oasis of peace, full of the love and tenderness of God who became human, allows us to assume the beauty of God at the very heart of our being, and reflect Him to all we meet every day of our lives.

////////////

Let us spend our entire life celebrating the Eucharist and being in the presence of the Most Blessed Sacrament. For a member of the Family of the Holy Apostles, the Eucharist is the focus of his whole life, his being, his thoughts, his activities. If at each moment, we try to do the will of God in union with Jesus, we participate each moment in the Eucharist that is being celebrated continually on the altars somewhere in the world (RV2, p. 249).

*I*n 1930, Father Menard at the age of 14 thought of joining the priesthood. A priest at the seminary gave him a picture of the Sacred Heart, *a very precious object I often contemplated and kept for a long time.* This priest who consecrated his young students to the Sacred Heart used to pray: "Learn from me, for I am meek and humble of heart" (Mt 11:29). "Eucharistic heart of Jesus, grow within me." During a moment of sharing, he said: *This teaching, like drizzle soaking into the earth, became a part of my life.* As a subject of his frequent meditation, this picture *helped him greatly to discover that God is love, Jesus Christ is love, a Christian is love, the Christian-priest is love and, more than anyone else, he must be a visible symbol of love by whom he is and what he lives for!* Each day of his life, he renewed his consecration to the Sacred Heart of Jesus (RRS, p. 1).

As as assembly of Christians (RV1, p. 17), a perfect place for the reception and understanding of Holy Scripture, sacrament of our faith, prophetic herald of our salvation (1 Co 11:23–26), the Eucharist is the *treasure of treasures,* the *centre* and the *summit* of Father Menard's life (TS, p. 30). His faith is boundless in the power

of the mystery of the Eucharist, the mystery
of faith, mystery of hope, mystery of love (RS
#41–43). A single Mass has infinite value: *My
brother priest, celebrate the Eucharist as if it were
your first and last time* (RV2, p. 240).

His great love for Jesus Christ and for priests,
never downplayed by sufferings, Father Menard
was firmly convinced that the priest is the only
human being who can celebrate the Eucharist,
that the Eucharist is at the heart of the Church
and that the Eucharist is the crowning point, the
triumph of all creation. Without the priest, there
is no Eucharist. *There is so much love emanating
from the Altar when the priest celebrates the Eucharist,
that even if the world were a thousand times more sin-
ful, love is stronger than hate* (CF 80). He repeated:
*There is love in the Church and there is love in the
world because there is Jesus Christ in the Eucharist.*

Personal faith is the secret of a true priesthood. The communion with Christ lived each
day in the Eucharist is the climax of our existence. It is not up to us to invent this priesthood,
to make it our own. It is a question of continually discovering it and putting it into practice like
Christ and the Apostles did. The success of our
Christian vocation is found in a continual search
for a personal communion with Christ. *It is necessary that day after day, your understanding of this
mystery and your love for the Lord grow* (URV, p. 40).

Father Menard saw in our room, our house,

our town or our village, continents, the sea, stars, galaxies and the whole cosmos … extensions of the Altar where the Eucharist is celebrated and of the tabernacle where the Most Blessed Sacrament is kept. In union with the angels, the spirits, mankind and all creation, our lives will be a constant praise to God most holy. All Christians, laity and priests, all MSA consecrate their entire lives as a permanent, royal and spiritual sacrifice. They offer it as a perpetual Eucharist, a banquet of fraternal and substantial communion of Jesus Christ within his Church. "Come to him, a living stone, rejected by human beings but chosen and precious in the sight of God … let yourselves be built into a spiritual house to be a holy priesthood to offer spiritual sacrifices acceptable to God through Jesus Christ" (1 P 2:4–5).

Father Menard considered the earth and the cosmos as so many tabernacles where the risen Christ, true God and true Man, resides. His life with all its activities is lived in the presence of the Eucharist. Day and night, he is in adoration, thanksgiving, making acts of reparation, prayers of requests. His life is a constant prayer. Let my prayer come like incense before you, night and day (Ps 140). *For the role of a priest is to keep watch* (RV2, p. 247)!

At the heart of the historic city of Lima, on Cusco Avenue a busy and hectic street of the business world, is a center of perpetual adoration of the Blessed Sacrament that each day has received, for more than 425 years, hundreds of persons who spend a silent moment of prayer or adoration. In 1979, in accepting the responsibility for this place of prayer, Sanctuary of the Blessed Trinity, Father Menard had set the basic condition, accorded by the Archbishop, that this place would become the main center of prayer for vocations to the priesthood and for spiritual leaders among the laity that the Lord would give Latin America. Each first Tuesday of the month, at the beginning of the evening, a solemn Mass was celebrated for all vocations and ending with a prayer vigil of moving communal adoration.

Not far from there, on Junin Avenue, there is an ancient monastery belonging to the Discalced Conceptionist Sisters, *Hogar San Juan that* became a MSA center for vocations where, each day also, Christians stopped for a moment of prayer and adoration of the Blessed Sacrament. In a festive manner, every Sunday night, at 6:30 pm, a solemn Mass, led by young people, was celebrated. Most importantly, the procession of offerings involved both sharing and support for the community. In the afternoon of each first Thursday of the month, a solemn Mass was celebrated for vocations followed by a extended moment of communal adoration.

For Father Menard, these faith filled, dynamic and joyful moments, are a visible sign of *the Eucharist that helps one advance in the footsteps of Christ. It helps one to participate in the most radical moment of his salutary and redemptive death. And therefore, there suddenly appears the light of the resurrection, of the new creation* (URV, p. 47). *Nothing is sadder than a Mass where we have just received, and shared the common bread, all the while treating each other simply as travellers in a train compartment or spectators in a cinema* (ATH, p. 86).

At each Eucharist,
Celebrated with Mary,

The Holy Apostles,
Francis of Assisi
And all the angels and saints,
With all my brothers
And all the visible and invisible creation,
I prayed …
Or rather,
I made my own the prayer of Jesus,
For the whole human family,
For all persons
Of all ages
And of all times …
And also for the numerous benefactors
Encountered during my life on earth.
(TS, P. 33)

Reflection Questions

Is the sacrament of the Eucharist at the heart of my Christian life? Am I faithful Sunday to Sunday, to the Holy Days of the Liturgical year, and once in a while during the week? Do I appreciate that at every moment of my life and everywhere my human life takes me, that I am living in a deep communion with Christ and the Church? With that in mind, do I stop a moment to adore our Lord at a church, in nature or simply at home knowing that the Lord dwells within me ... and that he invites me to live in Him?

9
Witnesses of His Faith

Focus Point

////////////

Throughout the history of the Church, there have been witnesses known as saints who urge us to follow the Lord. How wonderful it is to know that these same saints intercede with God for us! May we discover one of these saints to be a kindred spirit to help us live out the gifts and charism we received from the Lord, for our daily living!

////////////

We need saints. The Church needs martyrs (CF 83). By their lives, they clearly prove that we can live the Gospel in spite of the constant struggle of the old and the new man within us. Thus,the Church places a gift before our eyes. I especially admire the first saint that Jesus canonized: the good thief. That is truly what we are: thieves, this

is what I am ... I love the good thief, the
patron and model of all the chosen ones who
were saved and who will be ... But watch it!
... let us be prudent when we speak of the
saints: they received everything from Jesus
(TS, pp. 41; 45).

*F*ather Menard carved his spirituality out
of the living faith of the Virgin Mary (CN
#6, #10), of the Holy Apostles, our models of
apostolic zeal and missionary awareness (CN
#35), of Francis of Assisi, Theresa of Lisieux,
Vincent-de-Paul ... and of Eusebius of Cesarea
for whom he has a soft spot, to the point of using
his first name in religious life. *All of them give*
meaning to our baptism, our real religious consecration
(RV2, p. III). All find their origin in the one true
saint, Jesus! *Tu solus sanctus! Tu solus altissimus!*
To solus dominus (TS, p. 40)! Saint Paul asked the
Ephesians to spread the news about the riches
of Christ Jesus (Ep 3:8). Proclaim Jesus, that is
our mission, what we must preach, always and
everywhere.

Not once does Father Menard fail to men-
tion the place Mary has, Mother of Jesus,
Mother of the Church, model of Christian life
and of his priestly life. *To live, to love, to adore, to*
glorify is to obey God like Mary did in every moment
and in all circumstances (RV2, p. 25). Mary's attitude of acceptance, reminds us that to love God

is to obey Him and to love our neighbor is to serve Him.

Mary is the model of his faith and of his total availability in doing the will of God. Mary is mother and educator of his spiritual life, a model of hope and of courage in union with Jesus crucified, a model of charity inspired by the Holy Spirit, a model of prayer and fidelity. Mary's life summarizes the whole mystery of the grace of God's people on the move. In all circumstances of our lives, times filled with spiritual and material dangers of all kinds, Father Menard invited us to confide our vocation and projects to her benevolent tenderness: *Let us cry out with confidence to Mary, this ocean of love* (RS #25–28)! The loving mother of Jesus and of each one of us, her sometimes rebellious children, always cherished by her, has a special place in the heart of Father Menard. *Mary will have a special place in your life. We cannot separate her from the Lord* (RV2, p. 266).

On October 26, 1961, on receiving the "Domaine Marie-Reine-des-Coeurs" (Mary-Queen-of-Hearts Estate), Marian sanctuary situated by a lake and in the mountains, from Madam Emma Curotte (1890–1961), Father Menard pledged the Work and the Society of the Holy Apostles to the Virgin Mary. On December 8, 1979, he renewed his consecration *as her slave, according to the spirit of Saint*

Grignion-de-Montfort (TS, p. 26). In several let-
ters written shortly before his death in 1987,
he speaks of Mary, in the same manner, as *The
Immaculate Virgin, The Seat of divine wisdom, the
Mystical Rose and the Queen of the Apostles. Pray
for us, for your priests, your religious brothers, sisters
and consecrated laypersons* (RV2, p. 33).

As a pilgrim in the Holy Land, Father
Menard went to Magdala, for in his heart, this
place is as holy as the Sepulcher of Christ. God
intervened in the life of Mary of Magdala who
had marvellous charisms, but had gone astray,
according to him. *O how patiently the Lord waited
for her, loved her. In her own way, she came and
poured perfume on Jesus' feet. She was honest.... She
was not a fake. She did not pray like an apostle. She
prayed like a sinner ... with her life that had gone
astray. We see great human suffering met with great
mercy. Jesus told her: I do not condemn you* (CF 83).

Today, in their lives, many people make
mistakes, because they do not know the road
of love. Jesus is the light, that has come into
the world for the whole human family. Many
are those who go through life adoring false
gods: money, drugs, pleasures, consumerism....
Instead of condemning our brothers and sisters, instead of excluding them, Father Menard
asked himself and his brother priests what kind
of a God do we present to them. Are we faithful *in proclaiming the Word of God? ... I do not*

condemn these people. Jesus did not condemn. Jesus came to save us (CF 83).

Father Menard was edified by this special friendship Jesus had for those who make mistakes in their lives. It is an invitation not to become discouraged, to remain confident even in the most difficult moments, for love will always triumph over hatred. He admitted to having a special attention for all criminals who converted because they resemble us so much.

As a member of the Administration Council of the International Institute of the Heart of Jesus (USA), he met many witnesses of faith during his trips throughout the world, among others, Dom Helder Camara, Mother Teresa of Calcutta and Archbishop Romero, Archbishop of San Salvador. Having spent a week with the latter during meetings in Santo Domingo, he remembered him as *a very humble and simple man who had the privilege of being assassinated while he was celebrating the Holy Eucharist because he had had the courage to tell the truth to the big shots of this world. A courage we sometimes lack* (CF 83). Among other great men of his time, Father Menard admired Gandhi and Martin Luther King. *They didn't kill anybody. They died because they loved* (CF 83).

The Kingdom of God is hidden and its marvels will become known only in the beatific vision. For Father Menard, *the greatest saints were not canonized. To be sure, there are great ones who are. But there are also great saints who are unknown. This is what makes up the beauty of the Church* (CF 84). *This man or this woman with a chronic illness and who never complains; this mother who works to the limits of her strength; this man who has been suffering a long time and who perseveres in spite of his endless struggle; this layperson consecrated to God and who lives the gospel generously in the world* (RV2, p. VII). He granted, a privileged place especially, to these men and women who resemble us, those great unknown saints who leave their mark on the Church: *men who have seen nothing* (TS, p. 53). They are all important: *this monk praying in your name, this leper who comes to see me twice a week.... Never forget that you are great because of the greatness of Christ* (CF 85)!

Give me, O my Lord Jesus,
Eternal priest,
The courage to follow your mother Mary
In her self-effacement,
In her obedience to your Father,
In her docility to the Holy Spirit,
In her love for you
And in her maternal love
For the Holy Apostles.
Allow me to live a hidden life
So that the apostles of today
May shine as the light of Christ
In the eyes of men and warm their hearts

With the warmth of Christ's love.
Amen.

(Prayer of Sister Marie Toupin,
co-founder of the Sisters of the Holy Apostles)

Reflection Questions

Which saint of the Church is an important witness who could help me grow in my faith and human development? Have I taken time to know this saint's life and spirituality better? How does this saint support both my human and spiritual progress? Father Menard awarded a special place to people who resemble us. He saw them as witnesses of the Love of God. Around me, there are numerous persons who give the best of themselves so that there is more justice, more truth and more holiness in their world. Do I know them? Do I encourage them?

10
A Spiritual Retreat
with Jesus

Focus Point

////////////

What is the main thrust of my life? There are so many possibilities made of roads and dead ends. In the course of our days, how many illusions are proposed by the society around us. What should I choose to succeed as a man or woman and be happy with the joy announced by Jesus in the Beatitudes? Inscribed on the soul by God, each human is given a mission, a vocation to fulfill.

////////////

Not only do we not have the right to maintain ourselves in spiritual mediocrity, but we have the duty to aspire to perfection … whatever our faults, whatever our sins may be…. So what if our daily existence is dull, that we only have

*humble tasks to accomplish, so what if we are
ignored by others and considered unimportant.
So much the better! The essential thing is that
our lives be totally impermeated with love, be
a real life of the Father's child hidden with
Christ in God* (TS, p. 61).

*A*n apostle in the world, Father Menard,
gifted with an infectious drive, challenged
people with his preaching and personal
encounters. *Dear friends, the mission of the priest
and the apostle, of the pastoral agent is an impossible
one! It is an impossible mission to which the Lord has
called us. We need the Holy Spirit* (CF 79).

Many people came to hear him speak of Jesus
at the annual conferences of the Father Menard
Foundation (Montreal) or at Sunday Mass at the
Retreat Center of Villa La Paz (Ricardo Palma).
On each occasion, he asked his audience the
question concerning the purpose of their lives.
He dared utter the idea that one or the other
among them had never stopped to ponder the
profound meaning of his own existence. *You
cannot come to know it without contemplating the
One who is life: Jesus. God wants to make us into a
masterpiece. He sent the Holy Spirit to mould us in the
image of Jesus. We instead want to remain a block of
marble, instead of becoming a masterpiece* (CF 83).

The Holy Spirit promised us, helps us to
experience the marvels of the beginnings of the

Church (Ac 2:1–13) and changes our hearts. He is our strength. He brings us peace and joy. He shows us the true meaning of love. He is the soul of the Church. He is the soul of every Christian (RS #20; #89; #90). Thus, we must allow Him to fill us.

Day after day, we must grow in the actual world surrounding us. He tells us that no one should be opiniated in what he believes to be the charism of the MSA Society, for it is a continuous discovery of new facets. It resembles a diamond. *The real fidelity to the spirit of the Society, according to* Ecclesiae Sanctae *consists in a fidelity to the inspirations of the Holy Spirit* (RV1, p. 7).

Father Menard never ceased proclaiming that Jesus is the life! Only Jesus can say: "I am the way and the truth and the life" (Jn 14:6). *Your life is his life. His life is your life. What he does, so do you. What you do, so does He. And what a beautiful life you have* (CF 80)*!* Whatever your state of life may be — layperson, priest, young or old, celibate, married, religious, bishop — whatever our trade, whatever our talents or weaknesses, whether we are happy or not, Father Menard proposed that we take the necessary time to meet with Christ at the center of our being, so to assess our human existence as well as of our spiritual life. *If man tries to find fulfilment in his heart in the crumbs of happiness the visible world offers, his heart will always be hungry* (CF 84). This very day, at his invitation, let us truly ask ourselves: where am I at in my life journey?

At the end of his life, Father Menard handed down, initially to his spiritual Family but also to his brothers and sisters of humanity, probably one of the most beautiful treasures, still little known that has yet to be explored, a spiritual retreat of four weeks with the objective of helping explore step by step the marvellous plan that Jesus has for each human being. I am not alone on this road to wisdom. In our daily lives, Christ, source of our spirituality, is my companion (CN #5). With Jesus, I am invited to discover that each human being becomes someone better, more than I could have ever imagined.

These four weeks are a road of spiritual growth, a path winding, and steep, that leads us at our own rhythm, to the ultimate goal of living like Jesus himself. How can we live a better life than by remaining faithful to the Gospel? How do we choose the road that will lead us to him who is the Life? Let us not expect the structures of the Church and the world to tell us how to work at our own conversion. He insisted we must first of all, begin by changing ourselves.

This retreat with Jesus is a time to fall in love. Father Menard offers 112 themes of meditation spread out over four weeks: 1st week, *To live in Jesus;* 2nd week, *To act in Jesus;*

3rd week, *To grow in Jesus;* 4th week, *To attain the perfect maturity of Jesus.*

Definitely, this desire for perfection will be reached at the end of our road in the heart of this world. This new birth — our Easter Sunday — will then allow us to fully put on Christ and live totally at the heart of divine love. Our Redeemer will open for us the door of his joy and of his light. Lord, behold, I come to you as a child who throws himself into the arms of his parents. I throw myself into your love that awaits me. In full confidence, I offer you my life.

Like the disciples of Emmaus (Lk 24:13–35) to whom Jesus recalled that his passion had been the condition of his entry into his glory, we are invited to focus our eyes on Jesus journeying with us. First of all, the road he traces for us is the most daunting, but the surest one (MP 60). It is a time of grace. It is a time of fullness of faith. "Were not our hearts burning within us ..."? It is the secret of every Christian life that is revealed to us, for in the most intimate part of each one as with the prodigal son, the experience of God's unconditional love is felt. "But now we must celebrate and rejoice, because your brother was dead and has come to life again; he was lost and has been found" (Lk 15:11–32)!

Just like the Samaritan woman (Jn 4:1–42), *the first missionary of the Church, sent by Jesus to* her village following her personal encounter with Him (CF 81). "Come see a man who told me everything I have done. Could he possibly be the Messiah?" With these four steps, we enter into the gradual discovery and the decision of our mission as a Christian. The greatest favor I can do for my brother, my sister is to help them like Christ would to discover, reveal and share his inner riches. Father Menard assured us that no one on earth is so poor as to have nothing to share with others and no one is too rich to receive from others and from God.

This mission is unique, a reflection of our frailties, a reflection of our talents and of our charism common to all of us through our baptism. To be Church together, as the people of God journeying in the presence of his love and of his tenderness, in the world of today. From the first moment of his public life, Jesus had only one desire, that of making known to each human being the true meaning of his life, by allowing the most intimate part of his heart to blossom into the true meaning of love!

O Mary, Queen of Hearts,
You meditated Scripture and
Accepted Jesus, Son of the Father.
Help us to accomplish all he asks of us.
With you, we ask forgiveness and healing
Of all the wounds of our lives.
Give us the Spirit of strength

92   Day Ten

So that we can stand when the cross
wounds us.
You who visited Elizabeth,
Teach us to love our neighbor.
Like yourself, we want to be faithful
To our vocation so as to enter in glory
with you.
Amen.

(Pilgrims and MSA prayer at
Mary-Queen-of-Hearts
Marian Sanctuary of Chertsey, QC)

Reflection Questions

Father Menard insisted on the importance of taking time for yourself, of stopping what you are doing, assessing what you are doing, cleaning up things, and forging ahead in following Christ. Where am I right now? Does my parish, monastic or religious community dear to me, my diocesan Church offer me time for discernment and/or spiritual renewal...Do I participate and profit for my human and spiritual development? Do I take the time to meet with a spiritual mentor, the parish priest or a pastoral worker, on a regular basis as a support to my mission as a Christian living in the world?

11
Love the Church

Focus Point
//////////////

It would take many volumes to tell the story of our Church history down through the centuries. Church history offers us stories that make us both laugh and cry. Father Menard urges us to love the Church with our whole being, our whole heart and in every circumstance presented to us.

//////////////

If the Lord allows me, I would like, for a short time, to prepare priests and lay apostles for the Church I love so much; to prepare dedicated priests, priests who love their priesthood, who as their years in the priesthood increase, their love for the priesthood and the Eucharist also increases in an almost infinite manner (CF 83).

*F*ather Menard considered the Gospel of Saint John as one of the most beautiful texts of the Bible. Unwarranted, God loved us first. Jesus speaks of the heart of God who loves us and who gives us the ability to love and to be loved infinitely. "You must be born from above. The wind blows where it wills ... but you do not know where it comes from or where it goes; so it is with everyone who is born of the Spirit" (Jn 3:7–8).

For him, the Christian has not yet really understood the magnitude of God's gift. *When we were baptized we received, as if grafted to our human heart, the heart of God who gives us the capacity to love with the same intensity as God does. And we continue to love with our little human heart* (CF 84). Certain the only rank remaining for all eternity is the one of love, does he not choose as motto for his first foundation: "Above all, let there be love"?

Love is demanding. An undemanding love is not a true love. To love and to be loved is the root of happiness (HOM 1). This is found within us and is discovered in the present moment offered us in which to create marvellous things. The secret of a life of happiness is simple and within the reach of everyone. God sowed it in the world of today (PVH, pp. 4–7). What is most important is to love Christ and to live with him for, as he says, in eternity, we will not be judged for our fortune or of our function. *Millions will disappear. Love,*

the Word of God does not (HOM 2). Our worth
will depend only on what our charity, our love is
worth (PVH, p. 3). *The Lord asks us to do ordinary
things with an extraordinary love* (CF 83).

Where there is love, there is Church. By this
sign, all will recognize we are disciples of Christ:
"Love one another" (Jn 13:34–35). The mission
of the Church is to prove that we can be happy
on this earth without money, just the necessary,
nor power but not without disinterested love.

Though he met Popes Pius XII, Paul VI and
John Paul II — accompanying the latter during
a whole week during his pastoral voyage in Peru
in 1985, numerous bishops and priests from the
four corners of the globe, Father Menard, with
the enthusiasm of a fiery preacher, recalled how
much the rich history of the Church is not about
popes, bishops, priests and saints. According to
him, the most important persons in the Church
are not, *a priori*, those who have the most important roles nor the highest ones, though these are
necessary for the Church to function well. But, *the
history of the Church is first of all the history of those
who loved till the end as Christ Jesus loved* (CF 83). He
insisted that the Church is neither a building nor
a temple. *The Church is a person: Jesus Christ. She
has her ministers and her faithful. Together, we are the
Church. All together, with the angels and saints. We are
but a small drop of water compared to Jesus Christ who
is an ocean, for He is the Church* (HOM 2).

Through baptism, each one receives the mission of bringing his contribution according to his gifts (CN # 127). Each drop of water becomes "One" in Christ and absorbs all his riches. On its own, *it is nothing. In Jesus, it is everything* (HOM 2). Each drop of water becomes the strength of the ocean. The Church is holy with the holiness of Jesus. Doesn't Saint Paul write that we were enriched in every way in Christ Jesus (1 Co 1:4–5)?

The Church is like a hospital where everyone is sick … everyone, without exception, says Father Menard. To become a priest, to assume responsibilities and render a service in the Church, the Lord continues to choose sinners as with the first apostles. *How aware I am of my limits and my faults! Jesus, meek and humble of heart, render my heart similar to yours* (TS, p. 63)! The world tends to forget that. The One and Only priest, is Christ (CF 83).

The life of Jesus was strewn with obstacles. The lives of the Apostles were littered with trials. The life of the Church is full of difficulties. Father Menard fears for *a Church that is not persecuted, a Church that does not have difficulties, because this Church will fall asleep in a false security based on comfort. It is quite normal for the Church to have difficulties and in the fields of the apostolate are where the difficulties are the greatest* (DRC).

The moments of hopelessness in our lives are divine moments, Father Menard assured us (CF 81). He faced moments of crisis, of abandonment and of spiritual tribulations ... moments of doubt, of thankless questioning in which he experienced rejection or indifference, where he accepted his incurable miseries, his great faults that he was unable to correct, his many sins, his acute sensitivity in the presence of those who were rude and ungrateful (TS., pp. 35–37). In 1962, there was his dramatic departure from Montreal. In 1985, he gave up serving his Latin American foundation (TS, p. 69). At the end of his life, as his health diminished, he abandoned all his projects. All these stages of growth were painful. Bishop Cimichella, Auxiliary Bishop of Montreal, a great friend of Father Menard, testified at his funeral: "The crucible of suffering was necessary to bring out all the spiritual richness of his heart filled with volcanic eruptions."

In 1960, he encouraged his confreres not to allow themselves to *be brought low by difficulties: stay united with God. Then your struggle against the powers of darkness will belong to Jesus and his victory will be yours* (MP). In 1982, he declared how *each blow we receive in life is a shove in the direction we choose to go. Difficulties, trials are not obstacles. They are occasions to dig more deeply into our lives, to rediscover certain new aspects of life in the Church and perhaps to become wiser in the decisions we make. For, if we removed all the stones from the road, we would destroy the road. So if we removed all the difficulties from our lives or from our apostolate, we would never establish any apostolate* (INT).

The Church that Father Menard loved most is a Church that prefers to sow hope rather than to cultivate fear. It is a Church that tells Christians not to fear death, for it is life that has been transformed. It is a Church that lights a candle of love, instead of cursing the darkness. It is a Church that knows how to forgive, for forgiveness is greater than a hundred years of fasting. He gives the following advice to a religious Sister: *We are never mistaken in forgiving. Forgiveness is a catalyst that creates the necessary tone for a new departure and a new beginning* (12 August 1976).

My God, my Father,
I trust in you,
Not because I am good
But because of You who are infinitely good.
Please,
Do not judge me according to my numerous iniquities,
Known or unknown,
But according to your mercy.
Look with benevolence
Rather on your beloved Son,
In whom you have placed all
your complacency

And the faith of your Church.
I am so much aware of my misery,
Of my numerous sins,
That I have but one hope left:
You, my God and my Father …
I want to hide in your Son Jesus
And throw myself into the arms of Mary,
my mother.

(TS, p. 11–12)

Reflection Questions

Each Christian is a living stone of the Church. From my viewpoint, how do I see the Christian community, my diocesan Church and the universal Church? Which responsibility can I assume to serve the Church and its mission to spread the Gospel? When I hit a rough patch in my life, which rock do I grab and hang on to? Do I use this occasion to deepen my commitment to life and my membership in the Church community?

12
To Humanize and Evangelize

Focus Point

//////////////

Down through the centuries, numerous witnesses have sprung forth in the Church and the world to remind us that the humble and the poor have a privileged place in the eyes of God. Every day in listening to the news, we discover the depth at stake for society regarding poverty and human suffering, and the sharing of our resources ...Humanize and evangelize are Father Menard's lungs of life.

//////////////

At the end of our lives we will be asked one single question. When I was hungry, did you give me something to eat? When I was thirsty, did you give me to drink? When I was without clothes and shelter, did you clothe me (CF 81; RS #110)?

*W*hile waiting with a confrere for visitors in an airport in Latin America, Father Menard was eating his soup when a child, a hungry shoe-shiner appeared. The latter asked him if he could have some soup. This young child, thinking of others, very quickly added another child, then another and still another … until there were seven, eight! Each one enjoyed his soup. This meal in a soup became a banquet of love in an airport. *I came away from it transformed* (CF 85). The Kingdom of God is like a banquet …

This banquet is possible for our faith is spirit and life. The Church is spirit and life. All that is left for us to do is to put on the vestments of glory of Christ himself (ETQA, pp. 5–15). All of us want to love and be loved, because the Lord made our hearts in the image of the heart of God (CSA, p. 2). *It is the heart of Jesus grafted onto our own heart* (TS, p. 55). During our journey on earth, we must do everything in our power to love our families, to love others, to love the poor. The more human beings own things on earth, the more it becomes difficult for them to know God. For Father Menard, money does not fulfill a man's life. What fulfills his life is to make others happy. What an immense privilege we have to be able to help, together, priests and laity, the littlest ones of this world. *A simple smile can save a life. It is the world that is being saved* (CF 80).

Welcoming the poor should be an honor for us because they are the favourites of God. Take care of the poor and abandoned, because that is necessary for our Christian formation, to the sacerdotal (priestly) formation of seminarians as well as to our missionary education (RV1, p. 6). *If the rich knew the privilege they in being able to give to the poor, there would be a jealous rivalry, an envy in looking for the most miserable to give them bread* (CF 85).

Father Menard asked each one to take the time to develop his interior life and to discern the motivation and value of his commitments and life choices. "The truth will set you free" (Jn 8,32). *Let us take the time to reflect and to discern in our lives, what is really important and what does not deserve our attentiveness; what is worthwhile that will improve with time; what is it that is worth an eternity. Let us take the time to pray, to think of Him who is at the center of our lives, of our actions. Let us allow Him time to speak to us, to enlighten us, to challenge us and permit us us open the Gospel on the right page* (BF, Summer 1981).

Father Menard's objective is *to humanize and evangelize all our brothers of the human family, in accordance with the the signs of times where we live* (RV1, p. 5), so as to realize the marvellous plan of God's love. The present world has an urgent need of a new Saint Francis of Assisi *to cry out everywhere, that love is not loved. Everyone is looking out for himself. Everyone is searching for happiness, where it is not. If only, every single human being asked himself at the outset of his life where he could be most useful according to his talents and better serve his brothers, for happiness comes by giving happiness to others* (CF 81)!

Jesus was attentive to the physical health of the people who followed him. The miracles are a witness to this. Likewise, on discovering the life situations of the populations of Latin America, Father Menard worked for more than 25 years emphasizing his refrain, "to humanize and to evangelize." Be the salt of the earth and the light of the world (Mt 5:13–16). Matthew 25:31–46 makes complete sense when seen in the concrete happenings of his life, from Quebec to Peru, particularly at *Hogar San Pedro* (Ricardo Palma), a hospital for patients with tuberculosis, Aids, different types of cancer and, a center for abandoned children. Each year, volunteers from Germany, Holland, Canada … lived an unforgettable human and spiritual experience with him. "Truly, I declare, whatever you did for one of these the least brothers of mine, you did for me."

The missionary goes forth to love and tell his underprivileged brothers and sisters that they are important in the eyes of God. *The greatest force in the world is Love: to love God, to love our brother* (CF 85). We must carry in one hand the Gospel with the cross of Christ and in the other, a piece of bread to satisfy their hunger. He was convinced that today's apostle must work jointly for the human, the social and the spiritual development of each person. *When someone is loved, it is wonderful to see him grow. Talents, possibilities appear somewhat like what happens when the sun shines, life bursts forth* (CF 81).

In his spiritual will, Father Menard affirmed how much he wished *to be present* to each one of his brothers, with a message of hope from the Lord.

To be present …

- ∞ *in the least of their needs …;*
- ∞ *to each one of those living under oppression, injustice;*
- ∞ *to those struggling to be better, that the world may become more beautiful and free in Christ …*
- ∞ *to each brother who is ill, hungry, thirsty, weeping, desperate, who wallows in a night of pleasures … that destroy him and … kill him, may he still hope in spite of everything; …*
- ∞ *to each young person so that his life be one of service, using all his talents and thus, as an inevitable consequence, find the happiness he so avidly seeks in this life; …*
- ∞ *to each senior citizen so that at the end of his life, he may remain joyful, enthusiastic, convinced that the harvest time is near and soon he will be home where this wonderful peace he so desires reigns; …*

- ❧ *to each religious family that it may truly be the sign of your loving presence in the world; …*
- ❧ *to each human family that it may live fully the mystery of love that unites Jesus to his Church; …*
- ❧ *to each country that it may consider itself different, complementary, serving others and never dominant, thus avoiding all useless conflicts, and especially all wars; …*
- ❧ *to each member of the Work of the Holy Apostles, … to the laity affiliated to our Work …* (TS, pp. 13–15).

This passage best illustrates the intensity of his heart, an apostle seeking to obey God in everything with joy and love.

He attained his greatest dream and is now realizing it in the eternity of the heart of God.

Lord,
Insistently and counting on your power,
I ask you the great favor of spending
my life,
Before my death and after,
Of helping to promote numerous and true
vocations to the priesthood
And of supporting my confrere priests.
Priests, your priests,
O how I have loved them!
How I love them still!
I want to love them, always …
And if possible …
As they have never been loved before;

I wish to love them with the very heart
of Jesus.

(TS, p. 10)

Reflection Questions

Be present...two simple words, but so difficult to live! In my neighborhood, am I present to the humble, the sick, the fragile, to those living side by side with me in my own family?

The greatest strength in the world is love. Do I manage to give some time to volunteerism, a couple of hours a day, a week or a month, according to my possibilities (talents, health and availability), thus answering to the needs of the most destitute of my city, my village, my parish?

13
A Parable for Our Times

Focus Point
//////////////

Every day, we race down streets and boulevards. We run to catch the metro or bus. We dash from one place to another often without noticing what is going on around us, right under our noses. What a chaotic confusion! What a crowd of harried stressed out people! How many people are simply indifferent to solitude, to violence, to human suffering? And yet, each human being is unique in the eyes of God.

//////////////

Don't look for a cathedral, don't look for a basilica, not even Saint Peter's in Rome! All these cathedrals and these monuments pale when compared to the most magnificent monument existing, that is the body and soul of a human being. You are the temple of God and it is within you that the most magnificent lit-urgy for the heavenly Father unfolds (CF 85)!

*D*uring a stay in New York City, accompa-nied by several theology students, Father Menard met Dorothy Day (1897–1980), an American journalist known for her public cam-paigns for the poor and the homeless. He heard of this woman of Protestant background con-verted to Catholicism who lived with alcoholics, the underprivileged, the rejects, in a difficult dis-trict of the city. She gave them thirty years of her life. Later he told us he decided, to visit her one evening, to simply listen to her tell him about the Lord.

Following this fraternal and spiritual encounter, night set in. It was around 11 o'clock. During their walk, Father Menard invited his companions to pay a visit to the Blessed Sacrament. All were surprised and told him that at this hour, in the heart of such a district, all churches would surely be closed. Probably, with a little smile, he told them that they would understand what he meant, later.... On their way, they met a man in filthy rags, and he told the students that Jesus was meeting them face to face: *Look at him. He is a human being. I want to talk to him.* Coming nearer to him, he greeted him and offered him a cup of coffee. Surely, this man would have preferred to drink something stronger than coffee! However, he settled for the cup of coffee so graciously offered him....

They engaged in a conversation. The man was surprised and asked Father Menard, "Why do you stop to talk to me? He answered him simply: *I am speaking with you because you are a human being like me. You are as important as I am.* Me? Important? I'm a pig! You don't know the city of New York! This is the pigsty ...

Great! answers Father Menard. Then *I am in a pigsty ... But, there is no pigsty right here. There are only churches that can be dirty. They are temples of God. But the most beautiful temple is a human being!* Oh, to be sure, it isn't Saint Peter's in Rome, Notre-Dame in Paris or Saint-Joseph's Oratory in Montreal! For Father Menard, a human being *is the most magnificent cathedral that God ever built that man cannot destroy....*

During the ongoing conversation, there were more cups of coffee that followed. When asked what happened to him in his life, the man told his story. I began to drink a lot. My wife threw me out. She was right. My children don't want to see me anymore. This is where I spend my time. I live with friends. I steal whenever I can. I spend time behind bars sometimes. They won't put me in prison anymore. I am harmless. I am a pig.

Suddenly, the man asked Father Menard who seemed to him a good and honest person:

What are you doing here with us pigs? At that very moment, Father Menard was explaining that the street person was just as important as he: *We are equals. You have worthwhile talents.*

The man looked at him a bit perplexed. Father Menard continued: *True, I don't know you. Perhaps you won't have time tonight.... But, I would like you to tell others, some day before you die, that you met a human being who told you that you have valuable talents. And that this man invited you, no strings attached, to drink a cup of coffee, and have a chat that was different from those you usually have with your friends.*

The man then asked him if he were Catholic. *Yes,* answered Father Menard, who wasn't wearing anything distinctive that evening. *And you, are you Catholic?* Father Menard asked him. Yes, I am Catholic, answered the man, adding: Are you a priest? *Yes,* answered Father Menard. At that moment, the man began to cry. The tears flowed....

Then he asked Father Menard how it was that a Catholic priest would speak to him even if he were a pig. *I am living my hour of adoration because you, you are the temple of God and in you there is a presence as beautiful and as great as what we can find in the Eucharist,* he answered.

Perhaps the man didn't understand much of his explanation, but Father Menard tried, the best he could, to explain what he meant.

After buying some aspirin in a drugstore for the man, to relieve his headache, they departed.

This hour of adoration actually lasted two solid hours. *It was one of the most beautiful evenings of my life! Even before knowing him, I loved him....*

Every human being is a mystery, a sacred story. Let us never forget that. Father Menard was convinced, deep in his heart that *the greatest power in the world and in eternity is Love. To harvest love, we must sow it. We must not wait for the other person to love us. We must love freely without expecting any return whether the other one deserves it or not. That's how it is: to love as God loves. Only God can render us capable of loving in this manner* (HOM 1). To resurrect with Christ, we must love like Christ. When we love with the heart of God, it is wonderful to consider what we can say to touch man's heart.

The place given to the little ones, to the weak, to the poor is a priceless gift bequeathed to us by Father Menard. *Our love of Christ must constantly overflow and show in our love for our neighbor, a love with no exceptions that welcomes everyone* (BC, Letter of 21 July 1960). Everyone has his proper place and is called to follow Christ. "Indeed, the parts of the body that seem to be weaker are all the more necessary.... Now you are Christ's body, and individual parts of it.... Strive eagerly for the greatest spiritual gifts" (1 Co 12:22; 27; 31).

Thank you Lord Jesus
For the 70 years of life
You granted me.
What counts in your eyes,
Isn't the number of years lived
But how they were lived ...
Preoccupied in doing your will, always
And in serving our brothers....
O God,
You made a diary of our lives:
Your divine hand has written
What we have accomplished
And what we have omitted,
You write our story that some day,
Will be read to the entire universe.
May we make it beautiful
Thanks to the power of your forgiveness.

(TS, pp. 72–73)

Reflection Questions

Which is my "parable of life" that helps me change my perspective of a person among my colleagues? How do I express my love for others; for every human; for all of life around me?

Will I visit my home city or village and sit down to visit them to better discover how my brothers and sisters of the human family really live?

14
A Spirituality
of Pentecost

Focus Point

////////////

The human being has always aspired to dominate creation and its resources, the world and its vast territories, humanity and all its beauty revealed in the rich cultures of peoples. New social, ethnic and economical stakes at play … new technologies of every type are presented to our world every day. Means of communication have never been so developed. Yet … how many people feel isolated, rejected, and left aside?

////////////

Soon, I will have but one manner of praying … I thank you, O Lord.

You are marvellous in all your actions. I would like to be present to all my brothers and sisters in the entire universe, speak

their language and tell them that God loves
them (CF 79)!

*H*ow can we not live the spirituality of
the Mystical Body, that Father Menard
handed down to his brothers and sisters of
humanity, that stands out in our ecclesial history as the beginning of a new furrow in a
wheat field?

For all of us Father Menard proposed to
forge our identity as man, Christian, priest,
layperson committed to a *spirituality of life and*
of action ... that would never lose the amazing and
explosive power of the first Pentecost (RV1, p. 30),
we are instruments in a universal symphony that is
beyond us and that submerges us (TS, p. 74).

Laborers of peace, an abundant harvest
awaits us. Aware of our responsibility as citizens
of the Kingdom and living stones of the Church
rooted in a world, that disfigures too often and
forgets the God revealed in Jesus Christ, let us
give *the Lord an occasion to perform miracles ... :* to
render the world more and more the Kingdom
of God. *However, we must believe that his wisdom*
outdoes our narrow human wisdom (CF 79).

Let us bring only Love along with us. Thus
the prophecy of Isaiah is realized for the
Church and for the world and quoted by Jesus:
the deaf hear, the dead rise, the blind see, the
lame walk, the lepers are healed, the prisoners

are set free (Lk 4:18–19). The Kingdom of God is here, so close, by our side each time we are a visible presence of love by the Spirit in the name of Christ.

The deaf, the dead, the blind, the lame, those lepers, those prisoners ... they are, at certain moments, each one of us. In troublesome moments of life, *don't say that your life makes no sense! What is lacking is perhaps a bit of light* (CF 80), it is the stronger sister or brother who helps out the weaker brother or sister.... Let us keep deep in our hearts this joyful hope of Mary believing that God is working marvels (Lk 1:49).

Let us proclaim with all our might that the world is beautiful even though there is suffering, misunderstandings and human dramas.... He who believes and lives sincerely within the Love of God, takes the first steps in serving like Jesus himself who washed the feet of his apostles. He takes the first steps of listening, in mutual support and forgiveness.

A Franciscan until his last breath, Father Menard always considered the Family of the Work of the Holy Apostles as his beautiful and spiritual Family that he served to the limit of his strength and loved with the very heart of Jesus. *If I had as many lives as there are members in the Work of the Holy Apostles, I would, by the grace of God, willingly and joyfully give them up for each one of them* (RV2, p. 333).

Throughout his ministry, Father Menard lived his commitments, one after another, in the real spirituality of the Mystical Body. He inscribed his entire apostolic mission in the footsteps of the first Apostles at the heart of the mystery of Pentecost, for together we are living the mystery of an always new Pentecost.

Already in 1956, he reminded us how *the first task of the Holy Spirit is to pour out love in our hearts. Let us open wide our hearts. Let us allow all our small selfish preoccupations to disappear, to die, to fade, and let us ask it of the Holy Spirit who in the womb of the Virgin Mary formed the first great Christian Heart, the Sacred Heart of Jesus. Since every Christian and every priest are like a Sacred Heart, may our heart, if possible, widen and take on the same dimensions as that of the Heart of Jesus. May it become an ardent furnace of love. Without words, without raising our voice, may we be so filled with Love by the grace of the Holy Spirit, that we may warm everything up, melt indifference, anger and hatred* ... (APM).

One of his last wishes before dying was to offer his confreres and close lay collaborators, a Rule of Life that would guide them and accompany them on the road of humanization and evangelization. For today we must continue to propose the power of the Gospel to the world, at the very heart of human realities as a project of liberation and development.

In the introductory text that accompanies the Rule of Life, Father Menard explained the profound meaning of this Spirituality of the Mystical Body or Spirituality of Pentecost in which he proposed that we should live our ministry as priests or laypersons in the Church. In this manner, he reached once again the foundation of the spirituality of Francis of Assisi:

A *Spirituality* ...

- *that does not seek to choose between the Church and the world but is preoccupied with taking care of the world and, as a member of this world, being a visible presence of the Holy Spirit that is pursuing the work of Jesus Christ.*
- *of universal openness that pairs consecration with permanence in the world.*
- *that avidly seeks new forms of holiness, new achievements of the Gospel ideal.*
- *that joyfully joins us to the sufferings and sins of our brothers, realizing that we are playing our part in the unfinished symphony of the Passion of Christ.*
- *that asks of us the requirement and necessity to live according to our charism* ... (RV 1, p. 30).

By boldly and truly entering with Father Menard the most intimate part of this spirituality of Pentecost and Magnificat, we are surely building our house on the rock and not on the sand. The rain will come. The torrents will pour down upon us. Opposing winds will blow ... for sure. But nothing nor anyone will ever be able

to separate us from the rock that is the risen
Christ and who, furthermore, promised us the
Holy Spirit, until the end of times.

Jesus
Who made of your life
A hymn to the glory of the Father,
Give me a soul that sings like Mary,
A soul that expresses itself
Entirely as a hymn of love and thanksgiving.
Magnificat!

A soul that sings
Because it is full of joy, your joy!
A soul that sings

By giving itself up to the happiness of your
presence.
A soul that sings of your goodness
And that wonders at the abundance of
your gifts:
You love us freely without any merit
on our part.
A soul that sings in the dark
Because it believes in your light.
A soul that sings
In spite of trials and pain
Because it is certain about your triumphant
Resurrection.
A soul that sings
In order to bring joy to humans, my brothers

And tell them they are saved.
A soul that sings to please you,
To render homage to you on its own.
A soul that sings endlessly
Since your love is endless.
Amen!

(TS, p. 26–27)

Reflection Questions

Today, more than ever before, the Church needs laborers to work in the vineyard. How can I answer that call? How can I give more, taking into account my strengths and limits, so as to be a living stone of the Church? Father Menard invites me to be open to the Holy Spirit, just as the Apostles were on Pentecost. How will I will call upon the Holy Spirit each morning to be my guide and my strength for my actions, my words and my decisions of that day? Aware my own weaknesses and strengths, am I content to be a modest light of hope and love in this needy world?

15
The Mission Continued ...

Focus Point ///////////

As a follow-up to the thought of Blessed John
Paul ll, the Church lives an essential moment in
its mission to the world-that of a new evangelization — to rediscover the beauty and the power of
the Word of God acting in our lives. What every
Christian aspires to, is to resemble Christ.

///////////

> *Remember we are quite weak and small
> to take up this giant task, but it is precisely
> through our smallness that God accomplishes
> great things. It is our poverty that he loves to
> replenish, and it was the empty nets that he
> filled with the miraculous catch. Life is an
> act of never-failing trust. We must not allow
> our weaknesses to bring about a loss of our
> strengths. The depth of my hope lies the depth
> of my misery ... (VNA).*

*E*ven before his ordination, at the heart of his spiritual life, the focus of Father Menard's life was guided by a spiritual plumb line. In 1940, at the age of 24, he wrote that *wisdom will dwell in him through love, silence and mortification* (RES). When receiving Communion, he asked for the grace to supernaturally love all those with whom he lives and everybody else, for the love of neighbor is more important than any kind of asceticism. *I want to love especially the sick, the wretched, the poor and the sinners. I never want to make fun of the physical, intellectual or moral defects of my neighbor. I want to spread peace everywhere, to conciliate the greatest number of enemies possible* (RES).

For him, there is no real love of God without love of neighbor. That is why, he encouraged us, in all circumstances of our lives, to live in union with God, Mary and the Apostles, in the unity of the Holy Spirit, insisting three times on the word "trust." We *must always and without hesitation, be ready to start over again. The Lord asks us to make an effort, rather than being successful. His ways are unfathomable. Often, our failures are our greatest success. We must never forget that the world was saved by the most complete failure, that of the Cross* (QAM)!

In a hurry, one evening, Father Menard left Montreal for Holy Apostles Seminary in Cromwell, Connecticut. It was on fire. The next morning, the newspapers announced that it was preparing to close its doors. On his arrival he found 75 discouraged students wrapped in white sheets, who he questioned about what had happened. They answered him: Father, can't you see what's happened ... the building burned down? *Yes, I understand!*

Father Menard, gathered them around him, and told them that this fire *could not have been more perfect! It destroyed everything! We have other rooms. Let us meet in the chapel. We'll celebrate a Eucharist of thanksgiving, for this fire was a marvelous event!* No sooner said than done.... He told us later that he was the only one to say this prayer: *Lord, I thank you for having destroyed this house. In a short while, we will have a new building!*

This Seminary burned down three more times. The newspapers announced its closure three more times. Today, it is one of the most important Seminaries in the United States, where hundreds of young people and adults are formed to be priests or committed laity for the dioceses and religious communities of North America. In 2010, the construction of the new Seminary chapel will be finished.

What I tell you about this Seminary is the same for your lives! When we tell the Lord: I give You thanks ... the Lord immediately comes to us and goes to work (CF 82). Be confident ... just go ahead!

For Father Menard, nothing will ever

replace love: not money, nor ingenuity, nor resourcefulness. Above all, he reminded us, every Apostle must love "For the love of Christ impels us" (2 Co 5:14)! The secret of all the influence of all the saints is that they loved much. Let us not look elsewhere for an explanation of these marvelous, but rare people. It is the love of Jesus that assures the discovery of new methods of the apostolate and guarantees its spiritual fruitfulness.

Lord, send us courage. The courage to pledge ... to persevere without foolhardiness. The courage to take the lead ... to be disciplined ... to have stability ... to adapt continually. The courage to be alone often and the courage to begin once more with those who just arrived. The courage not to become irritated even when left alone and to keep ourselves under control. The courage to find enough time to contemplate and pray (TS, p. 76).

It is our mission to walk in the footsteps of Father Menard who, throughout his entire life, radiated the One who was his Source. So many different people throughout the world were deeply moved by his love of Christ and the Gospel. He gave them hope in living, again, tirelessly showing them the merciful tenderness of the Lord.

It is our vocation to dare undertake the challenge of the Church of today with a spirit of abandonment to Divine Providence. Jesus tells us what he told his disciples: "Take courage, it is I, do not be afraid" (Mt 14:22–31)!

It is our basic objective as committed laypersons, couples, families, priests, religious, MSA ... to wade out into the deep waters of the world and live as the already risen ones wherever we are, for *we were born for the world. We are citizens of the world* (AGF 83). And this world, in spite of all appearances, is thirsting for meaning and fulfillment. *It needs Jesus ... to be loved with the heart of God who has something to tell them ... but they don't have the time to listen to Him. They have so many things to do, as if it wasn't worth while to take the time to listen to God* (HOM 1).

"I beg you, in the presence of God and of Christ Jesus ...: proclaim the word; persevere, whether it is convenient or inconvenient; convince, reprimand, threaten, exhort with patience but always aim to teach.... But you yourself, be composed in all circumstances; put up with hardship; spread the gospel, fulfill your ministry" (2 Tm 4:1–5).

Father Menard invites us to be bold in our living of the present moment , the today of God that presents itself to us, never forgetting that each moment of our life is eternally rich and that the *world of tomorrow belongs to those who announce joy* (CF 82), the joy of a new spring enkindled by the breath of the Holy Spirit.

My God, my Father,
For me, the face of this world is in the past.
I have run my course.
I fought many battles.
My life has changed but not ended.
It continues.
I have now arrived at your house.
The Father's family house.
Here, all have but one heart and one soul.
I would have liked to live as an eaves-dropper
in the after-life.
You judge me with love …
With your merciful love …

A unique and just judgment
That the earth does not understand.

(TS, p. 12–13)

Reflection Questions

The Holy Spirit continues to spread gifts in the Church and to awaken us to live the Gospel in our daily lives. As a member of the Church, am I convinced how important my own responsibility is to the spreading of the Good News? Do I allow Divine Providence, that rises before the sun each morning, to have the upper hand in my daily living? Father Menard convinces us to live a joy rooted in the heart of God. Can I assert that I am a happy witness, zealous in my following of Christ and the Apostles, seeking

to spread the Good News of the tenderness of
God. Day 15 — Through thick and thin, I welcome the priceless gift of the presence of God
into each minute of my life.

Prayer to Obtain a Favor
through the Intercession
of Father Menard

Father, You who call us to follow Jesus,
We bless You for the work accomplished
By your servant Father Eusebe Menard.
You chose him to give many
Apostles to Your Church.
Confirm the holiness of this messenger of
Your Word
By granting us the favor we ask …
That through his intercession and by the
power of the Holy Spirit,
We may work for the awakening of vocations
and the formation
Of ministers in the Church and
for the world.
We ask this of You, God of Love,
For ever and ever. Amen.

(For all favors obtained
Inform the Secretary General of the MSA)

Contacts

MSA General House:

Address: 8594, Berri St.,
Montreal, Qc H2P 2G4,
Canada

E-mail:
  infogen@msgen.org

Web sites:
    www.msagen.org
    www.multimediamenard.org
    www.multimediamenard.wordpress.com

Biography

Paul Longpré, *Eusèbe-Henri Ménard, un vrai fils de François*, Fides, Montreal, 2000, 106 pages (Spanish translation: *Padre Eusebio Menard, Apóstol de las Vocaciones*, Paulinas, Lima, Perú, 2005, 128 pages)

Available at:
Father Menard Foundation:
E-mail: info@fondationperemenard.org
Web site: www.fondationperemenard.org
Tel.: 514–274–7645 Fax: 514–274–7647

Religious bookstore of Marie-Reine-des-Coeurs Sanctuary, Chertsey (Qc):
E-mail: secretariat@mrdc-chertsey.com
Pilgrimages: pelerinages@mrdc-chertsey.com
Web site: www.smrdc-chertsey.com
Tel.: 450–882–3065 Fax: 450–882–3759

Other web sites:
www.missionariesoftheholyapostles.org
www.holyapostles.edu
www.msagen.org/colombia
www.msavenezuela.org

www.vocaciones.info
www.msaperu.org
www.msacan.org
www.madredeladivinaprovidencia.parroquia.org

E-mail of the delegation of Africa:
msaafrique@yahoo.fr

E-mail of the province of Canada:
secretariat@msacan.org

Also available in the
"15 Days of Prayer" series:

Saint Benedict *(André Gozier)*
978-1-56548-304-0, paper

Saint Bernadette of Lourdes *(François Vayne)*
978-1-56548-314-9, paper

Dietrich Bonhoeffer *(Matthieu Arnold)*
978-1-56548-311-8, paper

Saint Catherine of Siena *(Chantal van der
Plancke and Andrè Knockaert)*
978-156548-310-1, paper

Saint Clare of Assisi *(Marie-France Becker)*
978-1-56548-371-2

The Curé of Ars *(Pierre Blanc)*
978-0764-807138, paper

Saint Dominic *(Alain Quilici)*
978-0764-807169, paper

Saint Katharine Drexel *(Leo Luke Marcello)*
978-0764-809231, paper

Saint Faustina Kowalska *(John J. Cleary)*
978-1-56548-350-7, paper

Charles de Foucauld *(Michael Lafon)*
978-0764-804892, paper

Saint Francis de Sales *(Claude Morel)*
978-0764-805752, paper

Saint Francis of Assisi *(Thaddée Matura)*
978-1-56548-315-6, paper

Saint Jeanne Jugan *(Michel Lafon)*
978-1-56548-329-3, paper

Saint John of the Cross *(Constant Tonnelier)*
978-0764-806544, paper

Saint Eugene de Mazenod *(Bernard Dullier)*
978-1-56548-320-0, paper

Thomas Merton *(André Gozier)*
978-1-56548-330-9

Henri Nouwen *(Robert Waldron)*
978-1-56548-324-8, paper

Saint Martín de Porres: A Saint of the Americas *(Brian J. Pierce)*
978-0764-812163, paper

Meister Eckhart *(André Gozier)*
978-0764-806520, paper

Brother Roger of Taizé *(Sabine Laplane)*
978-1-56548-349-1, paper

Saint Elizabeth Ann Seton *(Betty Ann McNeil)*
978-0764-808418, paper

Pierre Teilhard de Chardin *(André Dupleix)*
978-0764-804908, paper

Saint Teresa of Ávila *(Jean Abiven)*
978-1-56548-366-8, paper

Saint Thomas Aquinas *(André Pinet)*
978-0764-806568, paper

Saint Vincent de Paul *(Jean-Pierre Renouard)*
978-1-56548-357-6, paper